C]
ME
FIT

THE *Ultimate* CBT JOURNAL

A Healthy Mind & Body
Need Consistent,
Realistic Behaviours

Jill Bunny

Dedicated to CBT (Cognitive Behavioural Therapy)
and its ability to change the fitness industry,
one thought at a time.

CBT
MEETS
FITNESS
cbtmeetsfitness.com
Jill Bunny

THE *Ultimate* CBT JOURNAL

Welcome to the Ultimate CBT Journal! If you are anything like me, you may have an overload of notepads, sticky-notes, journals and random pieces of paper coming out of drawers, pockets and car doors . I have even found notebooks in the freezer. (Don't ask how they got there. I still don't know to this day.)

What I found frustrating was that I felt I needed multiple journals to track all of the things that were pertinent in my life. The result? I would stop dead in my tracks, feeling an overwhelming amount of anxiety. The thought that would come to my mind was, "Where do I begin?"

After months, ok I lie, YEARS of starting and never finishing a journal, I thought, *"It's time to make a change and create ONE that fits all aspects of my life requiring more of my attention."*

First, why did I have that thought? The truth comes out…I hit a wall—utter burnout. Unfortunately, sometimes it takes hitting that breaking point to make a change. I do not regret hitting that point—because it allowed me to sit down and create a personalized journal. I had no intention of sharing this with anyone. It was a personal journal that helped me heal and gave me strength, purpose and focus.

A few months into journalling, people started to notice changes—both physical and mental. People would ask, "What are you doing differently?" Did you change your diet? Do you have a new training methodology?"

The answer—I began to put myself as a priority. I looked at all the factors that were contributing to my "busy brain" and overwhelming symptoms of anxiety. The main culprit? Technology. (I have to laugh. I'm using it right now to do this… that doesn't make me a hypocrite, right?)

I found that my brain couldn't keep up with the speed of technology. We can access everything in seconds. I felt that I couldn't escape and just let myself "breathe".

Out of all the technology devices, I found that my phone was doing the most damage to my mental state. Although the phone is actually just a tool, somehow over a few years, I became the tool in the equation. I said, "ENOUGH IS ENOUGH!" I turned my phone OFF for the first time in 3 years (Other than for system updates of course). I felt a weight lift off my chest, and realized a new found hope. I could think clearer and could dig deep into who I really wanted to be. This led me to starting this journal.

I wanted to implement a digital detox plan each night, by turning off all technology items at a set time. But there was a problem: my phone was my alarm clock. For a split second, I thought, "I can't turn my phone off. I need it for my alarm!" LEGIT! Seconds later, I laughed and thought, "How can I solve this problem? BUY AN ALARM CLOCK!" Thanks to Amazon Prime, it came the next day, and my new digital detox routine was set!

Ok, so you might be thinking, "What are you blabbing on about and how does it have anything to do with the Ultimate Journal?" Well, let me ask you this, *"In the back of your mind, do you have the thought that you don't have time to journal?"* If you do, I have a game changing solution—turn your digital items OFF & see how much FREE TIME you create! By disconnecting from the digital world, you WILL be able to make time in your day to journal.

So, that said, I welcome you to YOUR SACRED SOURCE—a little exercise book to help you start and end every day. No matter where you are, or how the day unfolds, you have this book to help you keep yourself accountable; a little part of me wrapped around you.

The tools in this book will help you succeed—but you have to put in the time and work.

Are you ready to take control of your health and fitness goals in a systematic way? This journal symbolizes that one missing puzzle piece. Your jigsaw puzzle can now be put together, and the final masterpiece will be created! All you have to do now, is believe in yourself and stay consistent!

Four weeks of journalling begins!

Lots of Love,

Jill Bunny

INSIDE THE *Ultimate* CBT JOURNAL

LET'S GET *Started!*

In order to achieve ultimate journalling success, there are a few things that we need to do first:

- ★ Find or purchase your favourite pen or pencil that will be your journalling ONLY pen!
- ★ Create a safe space where you will go to fill out your journal. I recommend a quiet room, away from the kitchen or technology. (Bathroom, bedroom and car are all great spots for journalling.)
- ★ Find a place where you will keep the journal SAFE and out of others' hands. This is where you will brain dump a lot of personal things. So, make sure that you leave it in a comfortable, safe spot; or you can carry it with you in your purse.
- ★ Create a card or note in your bathroom that says:

  JOURNAL!

  That way, you are reminded to write in the book morning and night. (Create a new habit of journalling around an old habit—brushing your teeth. No way you can forget now!)
- ★ Set out 10 minutes in the morning and 10 minutes in the evening to journal.
- ★ Sign the commitment contract.

THE PLEDGE

Welcome To Your Ultimate CBT Journal!

Exciting news! You are now embarking on a brand NEW health & fitness journey with the implementation of the Ultimate CBT Journal! You are setting yourself up for ULTIMATE success because you are creating a new habit of reducing time spent in the digital world—and replacing it with the Ultimate CBT Journal!

You are going to create the mind and body you have been working so hard for, and it all starts with one thing...commitment! By signing below, you are committing yourself to filling out the journal as part of your DAILY routine! You will take your time, and be 100% honest with your answers! Let the transformation BEGIN!

Lots of Love,

Jill Bunny

My Commitment to the Ultimate CBT Journal

- [ ] I will answer each question truthfully.
- [ ] I will make time each day in my schedule to make the journal entries.

Name: ______________________

Date Starting: ______________________

Journal Time AM: ______________________

Journal Time PM: ______________________

______________________ ______________________

Signature Date

QUESTIONS *for you!*

Why did I choose to purchase the Ultimate CBT Journal?	
If I could achieve anything I wished for when it comes to health and fitness, what would it be?	
What would my ultimate achievement be in the next 4 weeks?	
How important is achieving this goal?	
How hard am I prepared to work to achieve my goal?	
What do I need most from **myself** to ensure I'm giving 100% towards achieving my goal?	
What do I need most from my **family** to ensure I'm giving 100% towards achieving my goal?	
What are the physical things I do really well?	

What are the mental things I do really well?	
How does my work help my goal?	
How can I make the most out of each training session?	
How can I help my family & friends with their health and fitness goals?	
What do I need to do to make sure I'm physically prepared each day?	
What gets in the way of me doing my best?	
What foods make me feel sleepy?	
What foods make me feel vibrant and energetic?	
How do I know if my recovery is working?	

Where does my confidence come from?	
How do I feel after I make a mistake? (Yes, we all make mistakes.)	
How do I behave after I make a mistake?	
Where does "pressure" come from?	
How do I feel when I'm under pressure?	
How do I behave when I'm under pressure?	
How would I know if I'm doing too much?	
What is it about health and fitness that brings me the most joy?	
What am I going to change tomorrow to make me better than I was today?	

MY GOAL

In **28 days**, the goal I will accomplish is:

The advantages of achieving this goal are:

When I achieve this goal, I will reward myself with:

WHAT I SEE IN THE MIRROR

We can express a lot of things though artistic expression. Do not worry about being the "best artist". Drawing out your thoughts, feelings and perceptions activates a different part of the brain that is not easily expressed through verbal communication.

In the space below, draw a self portrait. From head to toe, draw what you perceive yourself to be.

MY TYPICAL DAY

EXAMPLE

	Time	
	4am	
	5am	
Wake up.	6am	
	7am	Get myself and kids ready.
	8am	Commute to work.
	9am	Drive-thru (food)
Work	10am	
	11am	
	12pm	Lunch Break
Work	1pm	Surf Social Media
	2pm	
	3pm	
	4pm	Commute home.
Spend time with kids.	5pm	Pick up kids.
Fast Food or cook quick meal	6pm	
Chores Social Media or TV	7pm	
	8pm	Put kids to bed.
	9pm	Netflix
	10pm	
Bedtime	11pm	
	12am	
	1am	
	2am	
	3am	

MY TYPICAL DAY

COMPLETE SHOWING YOUR TYPICAL DAY

4am
5am
6am
7am
8am
9am
10am
11am
12pm
1pm
2pm
3pm
4pm
5pm
6pm
7pm
8pm
9pm
10pm
11pm
12am
1am
2am
3am

MY IDEAL DAY

EXAMPLE

	4am	
Wake up & Workout. →	5am	
Journal, Breakfast, Coffee	6am	
	7am	Get myself and kids ready.
	8am	Commute to work.
Work	9am	
	10am	
	11am	
	12pm	← Lunch Break
Work	1pm	Go for walk.
	2pm	
	3pm	
	4pm	← Commute home.
Spend time with kids. →	5pm	Pick up kids.
Make Dinner / Food Prep.		
Chores	6pm	
Social Media, 15 mins		
Organize Tomorrow's Clothing.	7pm	
	8pm	← Put kids to bed.
	9pm	Tea & Journal
	10pm	Netflix or Read, 30-45 mins
Wind down, Bedtime	11pm	
	12am	
	1am	
	2am	
	3am	

MY IDEAL DAY

COMPLETE SHOWING YOUR IDEAL DAY

4am

5am

6am

7am

8am

9am

10am

11am

12pm

1pm

2pm

3pm

4pm

5pm

6pm

7pm

8pm

9pm

10pm

11pm

12am

1am

2am

3am

DAILY JOURNAL *Samples*

GOOD MORNING!

14

Date: Oct 1, 2019

Hours Slept: 8

I am grateful for:

MYSELF:

Being able to provide for myself

OTHERS:

My children

THINGS:

My gym membership

In 14 Days, I Will:

Have lost 5lbs and have more energy.

Thoughts/Brain Dump:

In order to have more energy and be more confident and upbeat, I need to make sure that I am putting my health and fitness first.

Although I wanted to watch Netflix last night, I spent time with the kids away from technology, and journalled when they went to bed. This morning, I woke up with more energy!

Today, I plan on executing the same activities in the evening to see if this happens again!

14

TO DO LIST

MUST DO	BONUS	DROP/DELEGATE
Go to the gym.	Do laundry.	Bake cookies for kids fundraiser.
Drop off and pick-up kids from school.	Do previous month-end accounting.	
Prep food for next few days.		

TASKS COMPLETED	TIME START	TIME FINISH
1. Go to the gym.	6am	7am
2. Drop off kids at school.	8am	830am
3. Pick up kids from school.	330pm	4pm
4. Prep food for next few days.	6pm	645pm
5.		

NUTRITION

14

Meal: am/pm

SUPPLEMENTS & WATER	PROTEIN	CARBS	FAT	OTHER
multi-vitamin, omega-3, vit C, probiotic	5 egg whites	2 slices toast 1 banana	1 tbsp nut butter	coffee

Meal: am/pm

SUPPLEMENTS & WATER	PROTEIN	CARBS	FAT	OTHER
500ml water	1 cup yoghurt	1/2 cup berries 1/2 cup granola	handful of almonds	

Meal: am/pm

SUPPLEMENTS & WATER	PROTEIN	CARBS	FAT	OTHER
500ml water	chicken	quinoa	salad dressing	salad/veggies

Meal: am/pm

SUPPLEMENTS & WATER	PROTEIN	CARBS	FAT	OTHER
500ml water				coffee 2 cookies

Meal: am/pm

SUPPLEMENTS & WATER	PROTEIN	CARBS	FAT	OTHER
500ml water, omega-3, vit C, probiotic	salmon	white potato	coconut oil	veggies 3 chocolates 1 glass wine

14

TRAINING

Workout: Ultimate Training Program Vol II, Workout #5

EXERCISE	SETS	REPS	NOTES/WEIGHTS
BB Hip Thrust	4	12, 10, 8, 8	
BB Squat	4	12, 10, 8, 6	outside shoulder width stance
BB Step-Ups	4	12, 10, 8, 6	
Seated Leg Curl	4	12, 10, 8, 8	feet touching
Lying Leg Curl	4	12, 10, 8, 6	feet outside shoulder width

CARDIO	TIME	NOTES
Treadmill	20 minutes	12.0 incline 3.9 speed

Workout Notes/Reflections:

SOCIAL MEDIA AWARENESS

14

What or who were you looking at?

Found myself scrolling through fitness competitors' and food accounts.

How did it make you feel? (sad, mad, guilty, envious, happy, motivated, inspired, proud)

Jealous.....envious....depressed
I realize writing this that the accounts I follow are not helping with my self-esteem, and I waste a lot of time.

Was there something you did today that you refrained from posting online? Give yourself credit and write it down here!

I worked out and completed my plan without having to take a selfie to let people know that I worked out. I worked out for me, without the need for acknowledgement!

How do you plan to use social media tomorrow?

I am going to unfollow accounts that make me feel worse about myself, and mute social media notifications on my phone.

14

NIGHT

ENERGY

1 2 3 4 5 6 7 (8) 9 10

MOOD

1 2 3 4 5 (6) 7 8 9 10

FOCUS

1 2 3 4 5 6 7 8 (9) 10

DISCIPLINE

1 2 3 4 5 6 7 (8) 9 10

NOTES:

Since sticking to my routine, eating clean and at specified times, my mood, energy, focus and discipline have increased 2-3x.

List 3 WONDERFUL things that happened today:

1. I sat down to eat all of my meals.
2. I prepared my food for tomorrow.
3. I went for a 30 minute walk instead of watching Netflix!

List 3 CHALLENGES that you encountered today (if you had any):

1. I felt a bit guilty for sitting down and taking more time to eat my food.
2. It was hard to stop myself from feeling the need to scroll through social media.
3. Kids had a temper tantrum about dinner - made them eat what I was making.

What are some possible solutions to these challenges?

1. Read my response card, "My health is a priority, and I deserve time to sit and enjoy the food I prepared."
2. Turn post notifications off and set a time to scroll through social media later on after work.
3. Get the kids to help me cook the meal so that they are part of the process.

TIME

14

Am I closer to my goal?

 Yes, I am! I stuck to my meals and fitness plan!

I have:

★ turned off my phone.

★ prepared my food for tomorrow.

★ laid out my work clothes.

★ prepared kids lunches.

★ filled out journal morning/evening.

★ completed my workout.

Final Thoughts:

By setting a schedule and sticking to it, I have found that I have more time to do more things than I originally thought was possible. I also see the impact social media has on my self-esteem, which is why I am going to create specific times to check it (and unfollow certain accounts).

My kids are having a bit of trouble with the new changes with the meals. But I am making sure that I take the adult role, and I do not give in. It will take time for the adjustment to happen, and by doing so, they will also feel better, and have more energy/less mood swings.

Look forward to having another great day tomorrow, and filling you in on all of the details!

2 WEEK

WEEKLY

How many days did you workout?	Four
How were your eating habits this week?	Good—had a few slip-ups and unplanned wine/ chocolate...but a real improvement from the week before
Did you skip any meals? (If so, how many?)	I skipped one meal - was stuck in traffic and wasn't prepared with next meal. (I learned that I will pack an emergency bar and bottled water in the car now.)
Did you over-eat/binge?	I didn't binge - but did have a few squares of chocolate and wine two nights.
How many alcoholic beverages did you consume?	Four glasses of wine
What was one thing that you did for YOURSELF that no one else knows about?	I am filling in the journal and writing down my thoughts. I have always been scared to do this, in fear of someone reading it... but I know that my health and fitness goals matter more!
Did anyone do anything for you that you would like to take note of?	My co-worker complimented me—saying I looked happy and energetic! She also bought me a tea because she knows I am trying to eat clean and stick to my plan!
How were your spending habits?	Since starting the journal and preparing my meals, I have saved over $25 a day on take out!

REVIEW

WEEK 2

List 3 things that went well with your food/water/training this week:

1. I was able to get in 2L of water consistently!
2. I controlled my portions and stuck to the plan 80%! Huge improvement
3. I got in four workouts! That is two more than the other week!

How will you amplify these things this coming week?

1. I will continue to bring my 1L water bottle with me and keep filling it up!
2. I will continue to log my food each day—this is really helping!
3. I will continue to lay out workout clothes the night before.

List 3 things that went well, outside of your food/water/training this week:

1. My kids are showing more interest in the dinners I make. They enjoy setting the table.
2. My co-workers are being very supportive—likely because I am happy about it and not complaining!
3. I have great energy and focus! It is spilling over into my productivity at work.

How will you amplify these things this coming week?

1. I am going to create a weekly menu so the kids get used to a routine with meals.
2. I am going to keep positive at work, and compliment my co-workers! I might even bring in a veggie tray.
3. I am going to continue to journal, meal prep, sit down to eat and be grateful.

2 WEEK

WEEKLY REVIEW

List 3 things that you struggled with this past week with food/water/training:

1. I found myself hungry because I was stuck in traffic - led me to eat more at night (wine and chocolate).
2. I felt a bit rushed at the gym - need to give myself a little more time.
3. I had to use the bathroom a lot more because I am drinking more water—up at night a few times.

My plan to fix these struggles:

1. I will pack some emergency bars and water for the car. I will do this for the kids too.
2. I plan to leave 10 minutes earlier, and not waste time checking social media in the change-room.
3. I will finish water a little earlier—might help with the nighttime wake-ups.

List 3 things that you struggled with this past week outside of your food/water/ training:

1. I felt the need to check social media - scroll way too much!
2. I found it hard to not want my regular fast-food breakfast some mornings - habit.
3. I had trouble going to bed earlier.

My plan to fix these struggles:

1. I will set a time to check social media later on - and unfollow accounts that make me feel bad.
2. I will remind myself of how much money I am saving.
3. I will read in bed, and acknowledge that it will take time for my body to adjust to the new bedtime schedule.

NEXT WEEK'S FOCUS

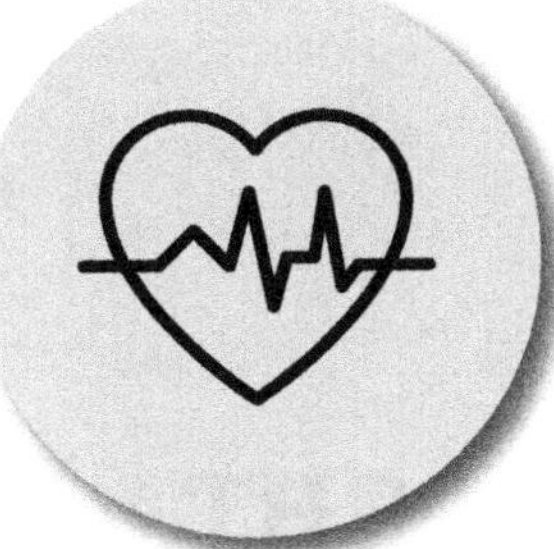

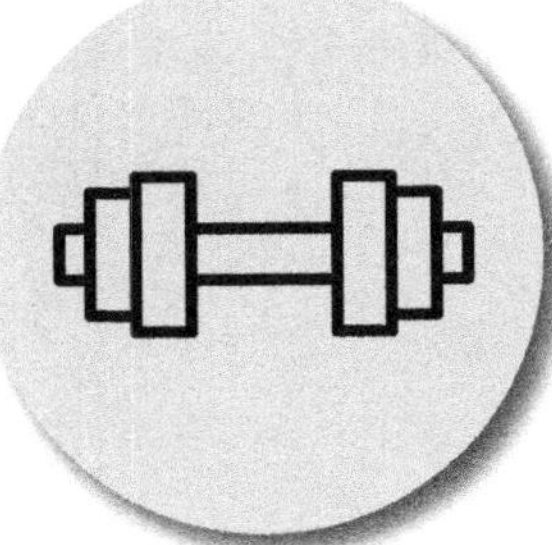

Fill out my Ultimate CBT Journal every morning and night.	Call my friend to catch up.	Go 10 minutes earlier to the gym.

I will:

Make my health and fitness goal a priority by sticking to my meal plan, getting in my workouts, and sitting down to eat my meals!

Plus... I will NOT give in to my kids' demands about food!

Notes:

"I am stronger than my excuses!"

Let's have another great week ahead!

DAY 1
Let's Go!

There is simply no magic bullet that will enable easy, fast and lasting health and fitness success. Instead of fighting against what you need to do, use that time and energy to just get started.

Every journey starts with a single step—so, commit to taking at least one step today.

GOOD MORNING!

1

Date: ______________________________

Hours Slept: ________________________

I am grateful for:

MYSELF:

OTHERS:

THINGS:

In 28 Days, I Will:

Thoughts/Brain Dump:

TO DO LIST

MUST DO	BONUS	DROP/DELEGATE

TASKS COMPLETED	TIME START	TIME FINISH
1.		
2.		
3.		
4.		
5.		

NUTRITION

Meal: am/pm

SUPPLEMENTS & WATER	PROTEIN	CARBS	FAT	OTHER

Meal: am/pm

SUPPLEMENTS & WATER	PROTEIN	CARBS	FAT	OTHER

Meal: am/pm

SUPPLEMENTS & WATER	PROTEIN	CARBS	FAT	OTHER

Meal: am/pm

SUPPLEMENTS & WATER	PROTEIN	CARBS	FAT	OTHER

Meal: am/pm

SUPPLEMENTS & WATER	PROTEIN	CARBS	FAT	OTHER

TRAINING

Workout:

EXERCISE	SETS	REPS	NOTES/WEIGHTS

CARDIO	TIME	NOTES

Workout Notes/Reflections:

SOCIAL MEDIA AWARENESS

1

What or who were you looking at?

How did it make you feel? (sad, mad, guilty, envious, happy, motivated, inspired, proud)

Was there something you did today that you refrained from posting online? Give yourself credit and write it down here!

How do you plan to use social media tomorrow?

NIGHT

ENERGY
1 2 3 4 5 6 7 8 9 10

MOOD
1 2 3 4 5 6 7 8 9 10

FOCUS
1 2 3 4 5 6 7 8 9 10

DISCIPLINE
1 2 3 4 5 6 7 8 9 10

NOTES:

List 3 WONDERFUL things that happened today:

List 3 CHALLENGES that you encountered today (if you had any):

What are some possible solutions to these challenges?

TIME

Am I closer to my goal?

I have:

Final Thoughts:

DAY 2

Let's Go!

If you feel like you have had a hard week, remember that likely not every minute of every hour of every day was hard.

There definitely were some hard minutes, but many other minutes were likely easy or neutral. Keep a realistic perspective.

GOOD MORNING!

2

Date: ______________________________

Hours Slept: ________________________

I am grateful for:

MYSELF:

OTHERS:

THINGS:

In 27 Days, I Will:

Thoughts/Brain Dump:

2 TO DO LIST

MUST DO	BONUS	DROP/DELEGATE

TASKS COMPLETED	TIME START	TIME FINISH
1.		
2.		
3.		
4.		
5.		

NUTRITION

2

Meal: **am/pm**

SUPPLEMENTS & WATER	PROTEIN	CARBS	FAT	OTHER

Meal: **am/pm**

SUPPLEMENTS & WATER	PROTEIN	CARBS	FAT	OTHER

Meal: **am/pm**

SUPPLEMENTS & WATER	PROTEIN	CARBS	FAT	OTHER

Meal: **am/pm**

SUPPLEMENTS & WATER	PROTEIN	CARBS	FAT	OTHER

Meal: **am/pm**

SUPPLEMENTS & WATER	PROTEIN	CARBS	FAT	OTHER

2

TRAINING

Workout:

EXERCISE	SETS	REPS	NOTES/WEIGHTS

CARDIO	TIME	NOTES

Workout Notes/Reflections:

SOCIAL MEDIA AWARENESS

2

What or who were you looking at?

How did it make you feel? (sad, mad, guilty, envious, happy, motivated, inspired, proud)

Was there something you did today that you refrained from posting online? Give yourself credit and write it down here!

How do you plan to use social media tomorrow?

2

NIGHT

ENERGY

1 2 3 4 5 6 7 8 9 10

MOOD

1 2 3 4 5 6 7 8 9 10

FOCUS

1 2 3 4 5 6 7 8 9 10

DISCIPLINE

1 2 3 4 5 6 7 8 9 10

NOTES:

List 3 **WONDERFUL** things that happened today:

List 3 **CHALLENGES** that you encountered today (if you had any):

What are some possible solutions to these challenges?

TIME

Am I closer to my goal?

I have:

Final Thoughts:

DAY 3

Let's Go!

"I really regret eating healthy today."

Said NO ONE EVER!!

Today, focus on healthy eating.

You won't regret it!

GOOD MORNING!

3

Date: ____________________

Hours Slept: ____________________

I am grateful for:

MYSELF:

OTHERS:

THINGS:

In 26 Days, I Will:

Thoughts/Brain Dump:

3

TO DO LIST

MUST DO	BONUS	DROP/DELEGATE

TASKS COMPLETED	TIME START	TIME FINISH
1.		
2.		
3.		
4.		
5.		

NUTRITION

3

Meal: am/pm

SUPPLEMENTS & WATER	PROTEIN	CARBS	FAT	OTHER

Meal: am/pm

SUPPLEMENTS & WATER	PROTEIN	CARBS	FAT	OTHER

Meal: am/pm

SUPPLEMENTS & WATER	PROTEIN	CARBS	FAT	OTHER

Meal: am/pm

SUPPLEMENTS & WATER	PROTEIN	CARBS	FAT	OTHER

Meal: am/pm

SUPPLEMENTS & WATER	PROTEIN	CARBS	FAT	OTHER

3

TRAINING

Workout:

EXERCISE	SETS	REPS	NOTES/WEIGHTS

CARDIO	TIME	NOTES

Workout Notes/Reflections:

SOCIAL MEDIA AWARENESS

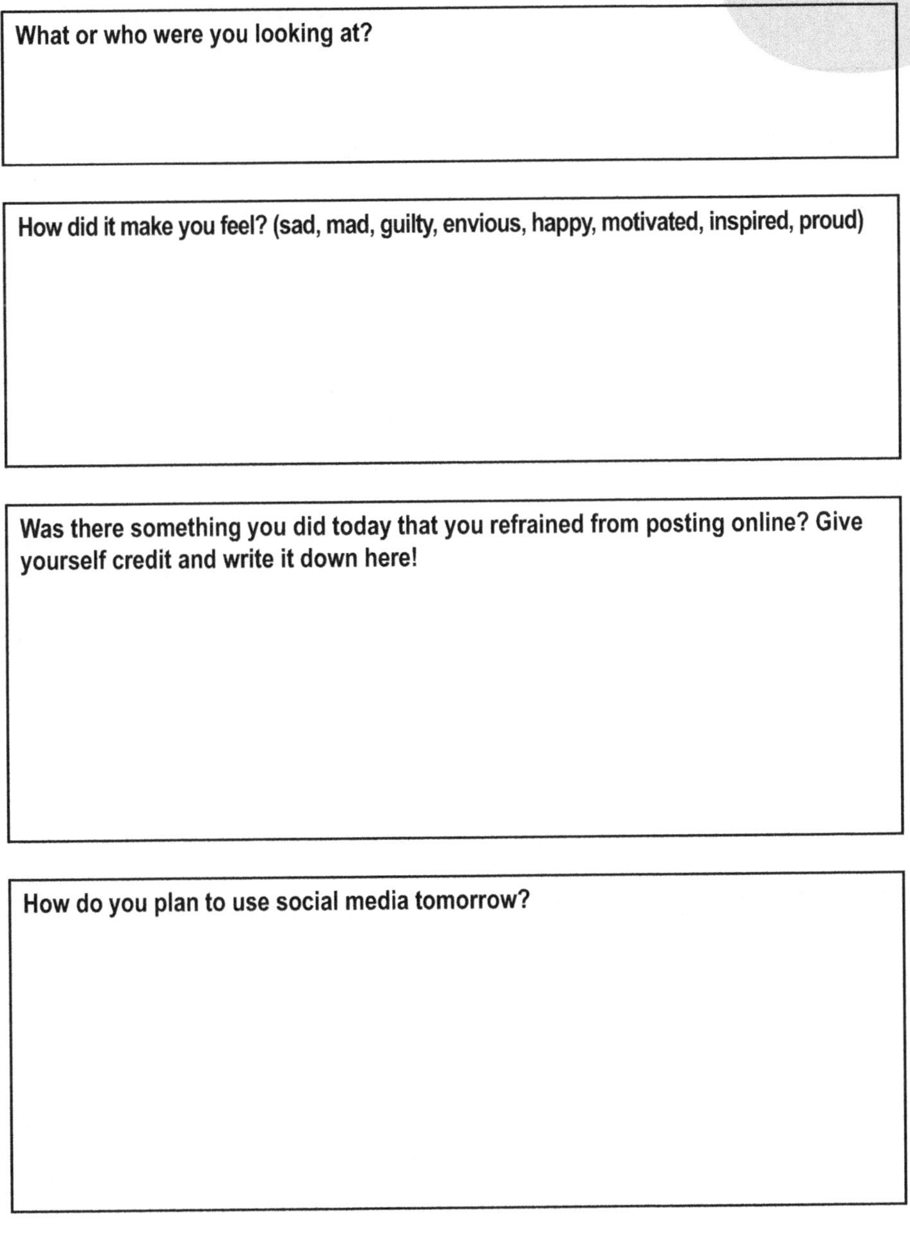

What or who were you looking at?

How did it make you feel? (sad, mad, guilty, envious, happy, motivated, inspired, proud)

Was there something you did today that you refrained from posting online? Give yourself credit and write it down here!

How do you plan to use social media tomorrow?

3

NIGHT

ENERGY

1 2 3 4 5 6 7 8 9 10

MOOD

1 2 3 4 5 6 7 8 9 10

FOCUS

1 2 3 4 5 6 7 8 9 10

DISCIPLINE

1 2 3 4 5 6 7 8 9 10

NOTES:

List 3 WONDERFUL things that happened today:

List 3 CHALLENGES that you encountered today (if you had any):

What are some possible solutions to these challenges?

TIME

Am I closer to my goal?

I have:

★

★

★

★

★

★

Final Thoughts:

DAY 4
Let's Go!

Remember:
If hunger is not the problem,
food is not the answer.

GOOD MORNING!

4

Date: ______________________

Hours Slept: ______________________

I am grateful for:

MYSELF:

OTHERS:

THINGS:

In 25 Days, I Will:

Thoughts/Brain Dump:

4

TO DO LIST

MUST DO	BONUS	DROP/DELEGATE

TASKS COMPLETED	TIME START	TIME FINISH
1.		
2.		
3.		
4.		
5.		

NUTRITION

4

Meal: **am/pm**

SUPPLEMENTS & WATER	PROTEIN	CARBS	FAT	OTHER

Meal: **am/pm**

SUPPLEMENTS & WATER	PROTEIN	CARBS	FAT	OTHER

Meal: **am/pm**

SUPPLEMENTS & WATER	PROTEIN	CARBS	FAT	OTHER

Meal: **am/pm**

SUPPLEMENTS & WATER	PROTEIN	CARBS	FAT	OTHER

Meal: **am/pm**

SUPPLEMENTS & WATER	PROTEIN	CARBS	FAT	OTHER

4

TRAINING

Workout:

EXERCISE	SETS	REPS	NOTES/WEIGHTS

CARDIO	TIME	NOTES

Workout Notes/Reflections:

SOCIAL MEDIA AWARENESS

4

What or who were you looking at?

How did it make you feel? (sad, mad, guilty, envious, happy, motivated, inspired, proud)

Was there something you did today that you refrained from posting online? Give yourself credit and write it down here!

How do you plan to use social media tomorrow?

4

NIGHT

ENERGY
1 2 3 4 5 6 7 8 9 10

MOOD
1 2 3 4 5 6 7 8 9 10

FOCUS
1 2 3 4 5 6 7 8 9 10

DISCIPLINE
1 2 3 4 5 6 7 8 9 10

NOTES:

List 3 WONDERFUL things that happened today:

List 3 CHALLENGES that you encountered today (if you had any):

What are some possible solutions to these challenges?

TIME

4

Am I closer to my goal?

✓

✗

I have:

★

★

★

★

★

★

Final Thoughts:

DAY 5
Let's Go!

Often people say, "Three months from now, you'll thank yourself for being on track today."

But guess what? Tomorrow, you will thank yourself. Tonight, when you go to bed, you will thank yourself. The good feelings from being in control or being on track start almost immediately!

GOOD MORNING!

5

Date: ______________________

Hours Slept: ____________________

I am grateful for:

MYSELF:

OTHERS:

THINGS:

In 24 Days, I Will:

Thoughts/Brain Dump:

TO DO LIST

MUST DO	BONUS	DROP/DELEGATE

TASKS COMPLETED	TIME START	TIME FINISH
1.		
2.		
3.		
4.		
5.		

NUTRITION

5

Meal: **am/pm**

SUPPLEMENTS & WATER	PROTEIN	CARBS	FAT	OTHER

Meal: **am/pm**

SUPPLEMENTS & WATER	PROTEIN	CARBS	FAT	OTHER

Meal: **am/pm**

SUPPLEMENTS & WATER	PROTEIN	CARBS	FAT	OTHER

Meal: **am/pm**

SUPPLEMENTS & WATER	PROTEIN	CARBS	FAT	OTHER

Meal: **am/pm**

SUPPLEMENTS & WATER	PROTEIN	CARBS	FAT	OTHER

TRAINING

Workout:

EXERCISE	SETS	REPS	NOTES/WEIGHTS

CARDIO	TIME	NOTES

Workout Notes/Reflections:

SOCIAL MEDIA AWARENESS

5

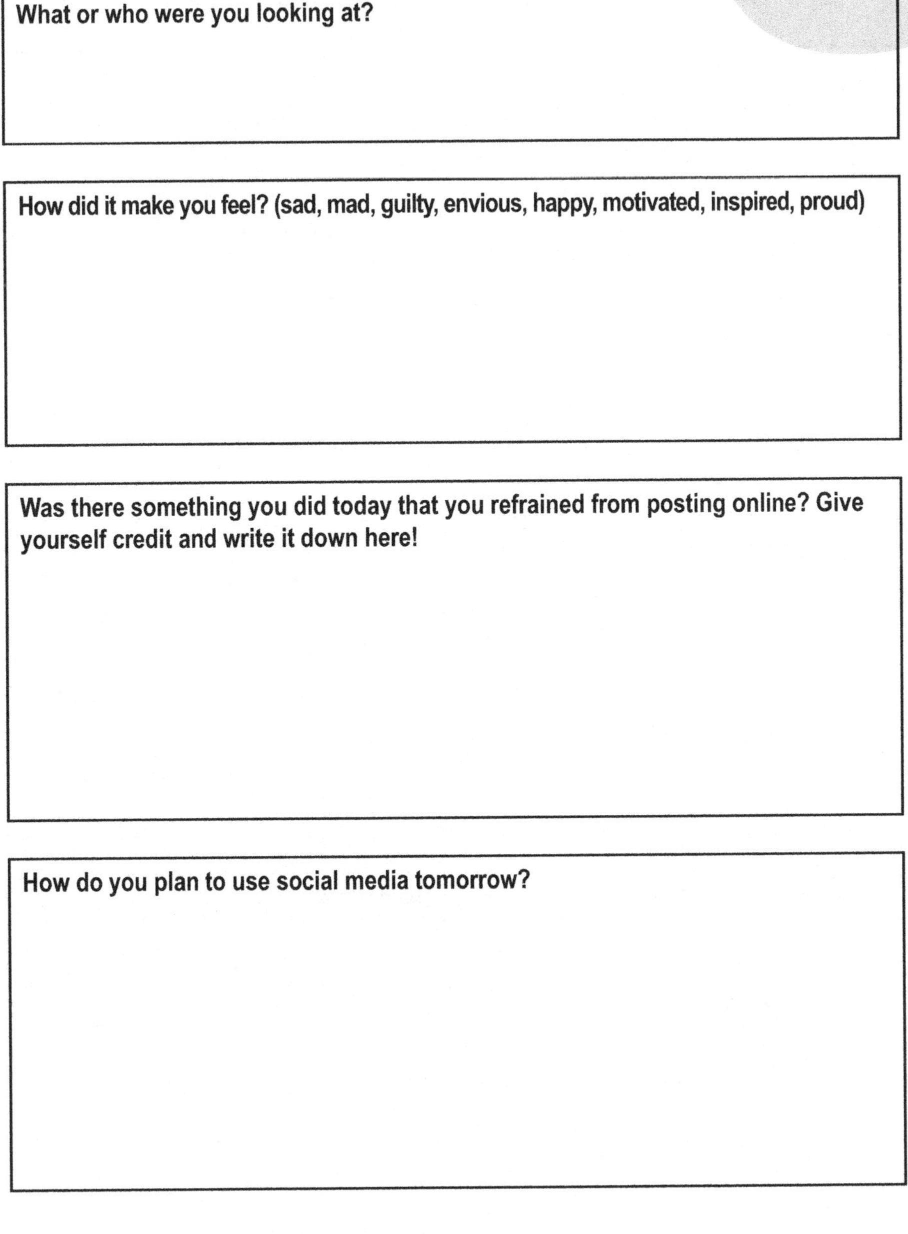

5

NIGHT

ENERGY

1 2 3 4 5 6 7 8 9 10

MOOD

1 2 3 4 5 6 7 8 9 10

FOCUS

1 2 3 4 5 6 7 8 9 10

DISCIPLINE

1 2 3 4 5 6 7 8 9 10

NOTES:

List 3 **WONDERFUL** things that happened today:

List 3 **CHALLENGES** that you encountered today (if you had any):

What are some possible solutions to these challenges?

TIME

5

Am I closer to my goal?

✓

✗

I have:

★

★

★

★

★

★

Final Thoughts:

DAY 6

Let's Go!

If you were driving on the highway and missed your exit, you would not think, "Well, I have blown it now." and continue driving in the wrong direction.

You would get off at the next exit and turn around. The same is true for health and fitness. The moment you make a mistake, turn yourself around and get right back on track.

GOOD MORNING!

6

Date: ______________________

Hours Slept: ______________________

I am grateful for:

MYSELF:

OTHERS:

THINGS:

In 23 Days, I Will:

Thoughts/Brain Dump:

6

TO DO LIST

MUST DO	BONUS	DROP/DELEGATE

TASKS COMPLETED	TIME START	TIME FINISH
1.		
2.		
3.		
4.		
5.		

NUTRITION

Meal: **am/pm**

SUPPLEMENTS & WATER	PROTEIN	CARBS	FAT	OTHER

Meal: **am/pm**

SUPPLEMENTS & WATER	PROTEIN	CARBS	FAT	OTHER

Meal: **am/pm**

SUPPLEMENTS & WATER	PROTEIN	CARBS	FAT	OTHER

Meal: **am/pm**

SUPPLEMENTS & WATER	PROTEIN	CARBS	FAT	OTHER

Meal: **am/pm**

SUPPLEMENTS & WATER	PROTEIN	CARBS	FAT	OTHER

6

TRAINING

Workout:

EXERCISE	SETS	REPS	NOTES/WEIGHTS

CARDIO	TIME	NOTES

Workout Notes/Reflections:

SOCIAL MEDIA AWARENESS

6

What or who were you looking at?

How did it make you feel? (sad, mad, guilty, envious, happy, motivated, inspired, proud)

Was there something you did today that you refrained from posting online? Give yourself credit and write it down here!

How do you plan to use social media tomorrow?

6

NIGHT

ENERGY

1 2 3 4 5 6 7 8 9 10

MOOD

1 2 3 4 5 6 7 8 9 10

FOCUS

1 2 3 4 5 6 7 8 9 10

DISCIPLINE

1 2 3 4 5 6 7 8 9 10

NOTES:

List 3 WONDERFUL things that happened today:

List 3 CHALLENGES that you encountered today (if you had any):

What are some possible solutions to these challenges?

TIME

6

Am I closer to my goal?

✓

✗

I have:

★

★

★

★

★

★

Final Thoughts:

DAY 7

Let's Go!

Being accountable for your actions is a critical part of your success because it enables you to recognize mistakes, allowing you to learn from them for the future.

It is not about making yourself feel bad for making mistakes: It is about learning from them to help you keep moving forward.

GOOD MORNING!

7

Date: ______________________________

Hours Slept: ________________________

I am grateful for:

MYSELF:

OTHERS:

THINGS:

In 22 Days, I Will:

Thoughts/Brain Dump:

TO DO LIST

MUST DO	BONUS	DROP/DELEGATE

TASKS COMPLETED	TIME START	TIME FINISH
1.		
2.		
3.		
4.		
5.		

NUTRITION

Meal: **am/pm**

SUPPLEMENTS & WATER	PROTEIN	CARBS	FAT	OTHER

Meal: **am/pm**

SUPPLEMENTS & WATER	PROTEIN	CARBS	FAT	OTHER

Meal: **am/pm**

SUPPLEMENTS & WATER	PROTEIN	CARBS	FAT	OTHER

Meal: **am/pm**

SUPPLEMENTS & WATER	PROTEIN	CARBS	FAT	OTHER

Meal: **am/pm**

SUPPLEMENTS & WATER	PROTEIN	CARBS	FAT	OTHER

TRAINING

Workout:

EXERCISE	SETS	REPS	NOTES/WEIGHTS

CARDIO	TIME	NOTES

Workout Notes/Reflections:

SOCIAL MEDIA AWARENESS

7

What or who were you looking at?

How did it make you feel? (sad, mad, guilty, envious, happy, motivated, inspired, proud)

Was there something you did today that you refrained from posting online? Give yourself credit and write it down here!

How do you plan to use social media tomorrow?

7

NIGHT

ENERGY

1 2 3 4 5 6 7 8 9 10

MOOD

1 2 3 4 5 6 7 8 9 10

FOCUS

1 2 3 4 5 6 7 8 9 10

DISCIPLINE

1 2 3 4 5 6 7 8 9 10

NOTES:

List 3 WONDERFUL things that happened today:

List 3 CHALLENGES that you encountered today (if you had any):

What are some possible solutions to these challenges?

TIME

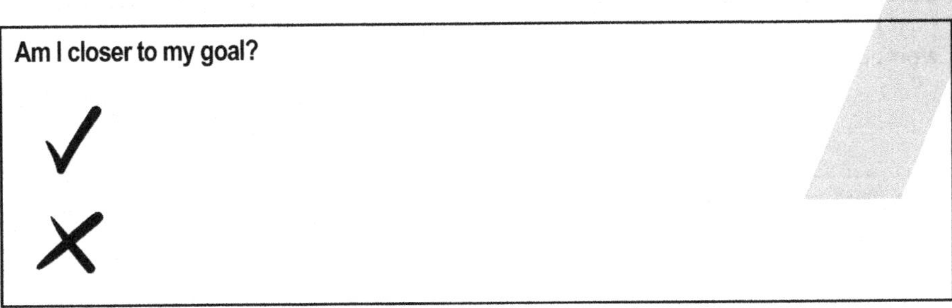
Am I closer to my goal?

I have:

Final Thoughts:

WEEK 1

WEEKLY

How many days did you workout?	
How were your eating habits this week?	
Did you skip any meals? (If so, how many?)	
Did you over-eat/binge?	
How many alcoholic beverages did you consume?	
What was one thing that you did for YOURSELF that no one else knows about?	
Did anyone do anything for you that you would like to take note of?	
How were your spending habits?	

REVIEW

List 3 things that went well with your food/water/training this week:

How will you amplify these things this coming week?

List 3 things that went well, outside of your food/water/training this week:

How will you amplify these things this coming week?

WEEK 1

WEEKLY REVIEW

List 3 things that you struggled with this past week with food/water/training:

My plan to fix these struggles:

List 3 things that you struggled with this past week outside of your food/water/ training:

My plan to fix these struggles:

NEXT WEEK'S FOCUS

I will:

Notes:

NOTES

NOTES

DAY 8

Let's Go!

Whatever you did or did not do over the past week is irrelevant now. What is relevant is what you do from this point moving forward.

No matter what, today is a new opportunity to have a great day.

GOOD MORNING!

8

Date: ______________________

Hours Slept: __________________

I am grateful for:

MYSELF:

OTHERS:

THINGS:

In 21 Days, I Will:

Thoughts/Brain Dump:

8

TO DO LIST

MUST DO	BONUS	DROP/DELEGATE

TASKS COMPLETED	TIME START	TIME FINISH
1.		
2.		
3.		
4.		
5.		

NUTRITION

8

Meal: **am/pm**

SUPPLEMENTS & WATER	PROTEIN	CARBS	FAT	OTHER

Meal: **am/pm**

SUPPLEMENTS & WATER	PROTEIN	CARBS	FAT	OTHER

Meal: **am/pm**

SUPPLEMENTS & WATER	PROTEIN	CARBS	FAT	OTHER

Meal: **am/pm**

SUPPLEMENTS & WATER	PROTEIN	CARBS	FAT	OTHER

Meal: **am/pm**

SUPPLEMENTS & WATER	PROTEIN	CARBS	FAT	OTHER

8

TRAINING

Workout:

EXERCISE	SETS	REPS	NOTES/WEIGHTS

CARDIO	TIME	NOTES

Workout Notes/Reflections:

SOCIAL MEDIA AWARENESS

8

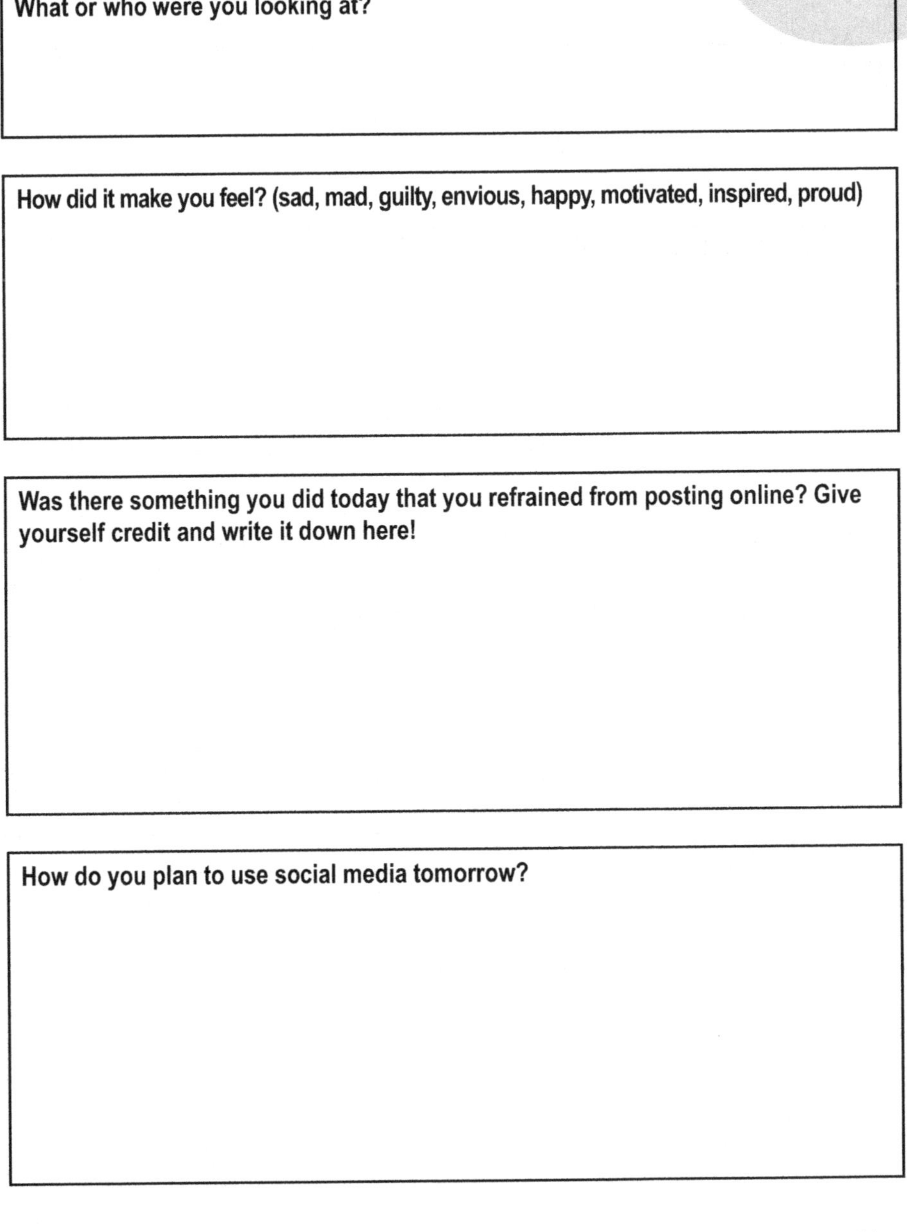

What or who were you looking at?

How did it make you feel? (sad, mad, guilty, envious, happy, motivated, inspired, proud)

Was there something you did today that you refrained from posting online? Give yourself credit and write it down here!

How do you plan to use social media tomorrow?

8

NIGHT

ENERGY

1 2 3 4 5 6 7 8 9 10

MOOD

1 2 3 4 5 6 7 8 9 10

FOCUS

1 2 3 4 5 6 7 8 9 10

DISCIPLINE

1 2 3 4 5 6 7 8 9 10

NOTES:

List 3 **WONDERFUL** things that happened today:

List 3 **CHALLENGES** that you encountered today (if you had any):

What are some possible solutions to these challenges?

TIME

8

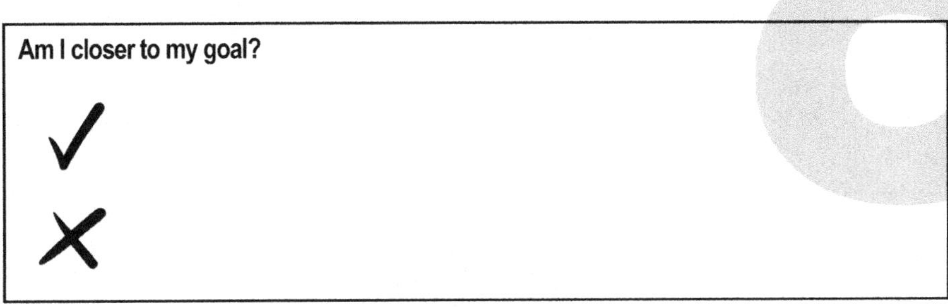
Am I closer to my goal?

I have:

Final Thoughts:

DAY 9

Let's Go!

If you are feeling discouraged by getting off track, remind yourself that you are capable of major change.

You can do this.

It is not always easy, but the most important thing is that you keep going.

GOOD MORNING!

9

Date: ______________________

Hours Slept: ______________________

I am grateful for:

MYSELF:

OTHERS:

THINGS:

In 20 Days, I Will:

Thoughts/Brain Dump:

9

TO DO LIST

MUST DO	BONUS	DROP/DELEGATE

TASKS COMPLETED	TIME START	TIME FINISH
1.		
2.		
3.		
4.		
5.		

NUTRITION

9

Meal: **am/pm**

SUPPLEMENTS & WATER	PROTEIN	CARBS	FAT	OTHER

Meal: **am/pm**

SUPPLEMENTS & WATER	PROTEIN	CARBS	FAT	OTHER

Meal: **am/pm**

SUPPLEMENTS & WATER	PROTEIN	CARBS	FAT	OTHER

Meal: **am/pm**

SUPPLEMENTS & WATER	PROTEIN	CARBS	FAT	OTHER

Meal: **am/pm**

SUPPLEMENTS & WATER	PROTEIN	CARBS	FAT	OTHER

9

TRAINING

Workout:

EXERCISE	SETS	REPS	NOTES/WEIGHTS

CARDIO	TIME	NOTES

Workout Notes/Reflections:

SOCIAL MEDIA AWARENESS

9

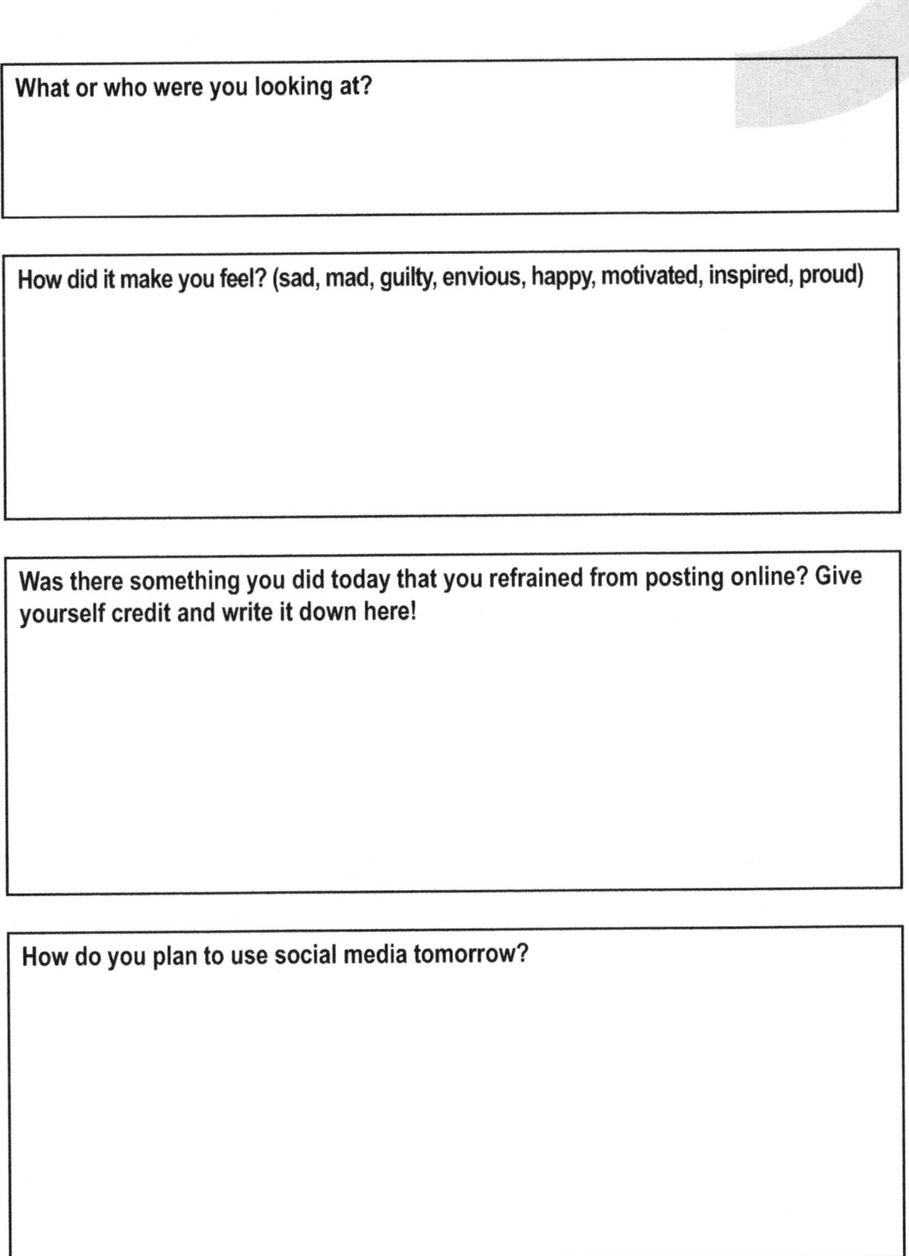

What or who were you looking at?

How did it make you feel? (sad, mad, guilty, envious, happy, motivated, inspired, proud)

Was there something you did today that you refrained from posting online? Give yourself credit and write it down here!

How do you plan to use social media tomorrow?

9

NIGHT

ENERGY

1 2 3 4 5 6 7 8 9 10

MOOD

1 2 3 4 5 6 7 8 9 10

FOCUS

1 2 3 4 5 6 7 8 9 10

DISCIPLINE

1 2 3 4 5 6 7 8 9 10

NOTES:

List 3 WONDERFUL things that happened today:

List 3 CHALLENGES that you encountered today (if you had any):

What are some possible solutions to these challenges?

TIME

Am I closer to my goal?

I have:

★ ★

★ ★

★ ★

Final Thoughts:

DAY 10

Let's Go!

The next time you know you have a stressful situation coming up, ask yourself, "How will I get through this without eating?"

So you don't end up turning to food, make a plan in advance for the ways you will deal with stress and anxiety.

10

GOOD MORNING!

Date: ______________________

Hours Slept: ______________________

I am grateful for:

MYSELF:

OTHERS:

THINGS:

In 19 Days, I Will:

Thoughts/Brain Dump:

10

TO DO LIST

MUST DO	BONUS	DROP/DELEGATE

TASKS COMPLETED	TIME START	TIME FINISH
1.		
2.		
3.		
4.		
5.		

NUTRITION

10

Meal: **am/pm**

SUPPLEMENTS & WATER	PROTEIN	CARBS	FAT	OTHER

Meal: **am/pm**

SUPPLEMENTS & WATER	PROTEIN	CARBS	FAT	OTHER

Meal: **am/pm**

SUPPLEMENTS & WATER	PROTEIN	CARBS	FAT	OTHER

Meal: **am/pm**

SUPPLEMENTS & WATER	PROTEIN	CARBS	FAT	OTHER

Meal: **am/pm**

SUPPLEMENTS & WATER	PROTEIN	CARBS	FAT	OTHER

10 TRAINING

Workout:

EXERCISE	SETS	REPS	NOTES/WEIGHTS

CARDIO	TIME	NOTES

Workout Notes/Reflections:

SOCIAL MEDIA AWARENESS

10

What or who were you looking at?

How did it make you feel? (sad, mad, guilty, envious, happy, motivated, inspired, proud)

Was there something you did today that you refrained from posting online? Give yourself credit and write it down here!

How do you plan to use social media tomorrow?

10

NIGHT

ENERGY
1 2 3 4 5 6 7 8 9 10

MOOD
1 2 3 4 5 6 7 8 9 10

FOCUS
1 2 3 4 5 6 7 8 9 10

DISCIPLINE
1 2 3 4 5 6 7 8 9 10

NOTES:

List 3 WONDERFUL things that happened today:

List 3 CHALLENGES that you encountered today (if you had any):

What are some possible solutions to these challenges?

TIME

10

Am I closer to my goal?

✓

✗

I have:

Final Thoughts:

DAY 11

Let's Go!

There is a big difference between things that are really hard and things that are impossible. If you feel overwhelmed by your goal, remind yourself that it is a matter of learning and practicing your skills. Telling yourself it is impossible is an excuse to give up. Telling yourself it is hard but worth working on is motivation to keep moving forward.

11

GOOD MORNING!

Date: ______________________________

Hours Slept: ________________________

I am grateful for:

MYSELF:

OTHERS:

THINGS:

In 18 Days, I Will:

Thoughts/Brain Dump:

11

TO DO LIST

MUST DO	BONUS	DROP/DELEGATE

TASKS COMPLETED	TIME START	TIME FINISH
1.		
2.		
3.		
4.		
5.		

NUTRITION

11

Meal: **am/pm**

SUPPLEMENTS & WATER	PROTEIN	CARBS	FAT	OTHER

Meal: **am/pm**

SUPPLEMENTS & WATER	PROTEIN	CARBS	FAT	OTHER

Meal: **am/pm**

SUPPLEMENTS & WATER	PROTEIN	CARBS	FAT	OTHER

Meal: **am/pm**

SUPPLEMENTS & WATER	PROTEIN	CARBS	FAT	OTHER

Meal: **am/pm**

SUPPLEMENTS & WATER	PROTEIN	CARBS	FAT	OTHER

11 TRAINING

Workout:

EXERCISE	SETS	REPS	NOTES/WEIGHTS

CARDIO	TIME	NOTES

Workout Notes/Reflections:

11

SOCIAL MEDIA AWARENESS

What or who were you looking at?

How did it make you feel? (sad, mad, guilty, envious, happy, motivated, inspired, proud)

Was there something you did today that you refrained from posting online? Give yourself credit and write it down here!

How do you plan to use social media tomorrow?

11

NIGHT

ENERGY
1 2 3 4 5 6 7 8 9 10

MOOD
1 2 3 4 5 6 7 8 9 10

FOCUS
1 2 3 4 5 6 7 8 9 10

DISCIPLINE
1 2 3 4 5 6 7 8 9 10

NOTES:

List 3 WONDERFUL things that happened today:

List 3 CHALLENGES that you encountered today (if you had any):

What are some possible solutions to these challenges?

TIME

11

Am I closer to my goal?

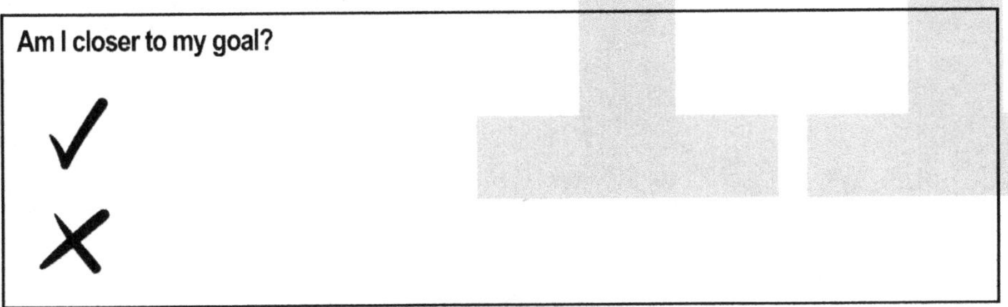

I have:

Final Thoughts:

DAY 12

Let's Go!

It is important to separate eating from exercise.

Exercise so that you can be physically and mentally healthy, not so that you can take in extra calories.

GOOD MORNING!

12

Date: ______________________

Hours Slept: ______________________

I am grateful for:

MYSELF:

OTHERS:

THINGS:

In 17 Days, I Will:

Thoughts/Brain Dump:

12

TO DO LIST

MUST DO	BONUS	DROP/DELEGATE

TASKS COMPLETED	TIME START	TIME FINISH
1.		
2.		
3.		
4.		
5.		

NUTRITION

12

Meal: **am/pm**

SUPPLEMENTS & WATER	PROTEIN	CARBS	FAT	OTHER

Meal: **am/pm**

SUPPLEMENTS & WATER	PROTEIN	CARBS	FAT	OTHER

Meal: **am/pm**

SUPPLEMENTS & WATER	PROTEIN	CARBS	FAT	OTHER

Meal: **am/pm**

SUPPLEMENTS & WATER	PROTEIN	CARBS	FAT	OTHER

Meal: **am/pm**

SUPPLEMENTS & WATER	PROTEIN	CARBS	FAT	OTHER

12

TRAINING

Workout:

EXERCISE	SETS	REPS	NOTES/WEIGHTS

CARDIO	TIME	NOTES

Workout Notes/Reflections:

12

SOCIAL MEDIA AWARENESS

What or who were you looking at?

How did it make you feel? (sad, mad, guilty, envious, happy, motivated, inspired, proud)

Was there something you did today that you refrained from posting online? Give yourself credit and write it down here!

How do you plan to use social media tomorrow?

12

NIGHT

ENERGY

1 2 3 4 5 6 7 8 9 10

MOOD

1 2 3 4 5 6 7 8 9 10

FOCUS

1 2 3 4 5 6 7 8 9 10

DISCIPLINE

1 2 3 4 5 6 7 8 9 10

NOTES:

List 3 WONDERFUL things that happened today:

List 3 CHALLENGES that you encountered today (if you had any):

What are some possible solutions to these challenges?

TIME

12

Am I closer to my goal?

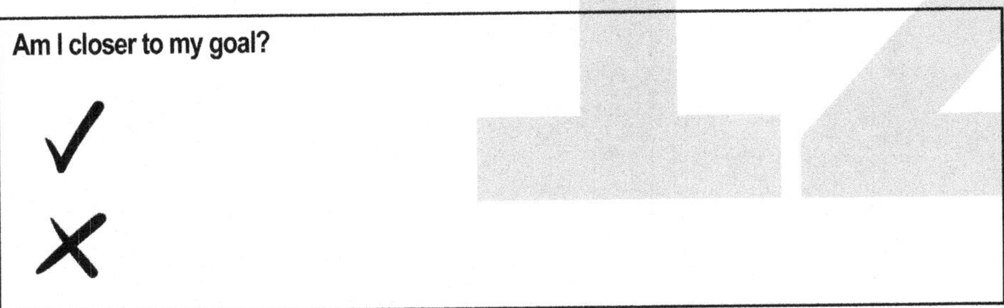

I have:

Final Thoughts:

DAY 13

Let's Go!

Today is an opportunity for a fresh start.

Starting right now, give yourself credit for every positive thing you do towards meeting your goal.

It will help you feel better, raise your confidence, and give you motivation to keep going.

13

GOOD MORNING!

Date: ______________________________

Hours Slept: ________________________

I am grateful for:

MYSELF:

OTHERS:

THINGS:

In 16 Days, I Will:

Thoughts/Brain Dump:

13

TO DO LIST

MUST DO	BONUS	DROP/DELEGATE

TASKS COMPLETED	TIME START	TIME FINISH
1.		
2.		
3.		
4.		
5.		

NUTRITION

13

Meal: **am/pm**

SUPPLEMENTS & WATER	PROTEIN	CARBS	FAT	OTHER

Meal: **am/pm**

SUPPLEMENTS & WATER	PROTEIN	CARBS	FAT	OTHER

Meal: **am/pm**

SUPPLEMENTS & WATER	PROTEIN	CARBS	FAT	OTHER

Meal: **am/pm**

SUPPLEMENTS & WATER	PROTEIN	CARBS	FAT	OTHER

Meal: **am/pm**

SUPPLEMENTS & WATER	PROTEIN	CARBS	FAT	OTHER

13 TRAINING

Workout:

EXERCISE	SETS	REPS	NOTES/WEIGHTS

CARDIO	TIME	NOTES

Workout Notes/Reflections:

SOCIAL MEDIA AWARENESS

13

What or who were you looking at?

How did it make you feel? (sad, mad, guilty, envious, happy, motivated, inspired, proud)

Was there something you did today that you refrained from posting online? Give yourself credit and write it down here!

How do you plan to use social media tomorrow?

13

NIGHT

ENERGY

1 2 3 4 5 6 7 8 9 10

MOOD

1 2 3 4 5 6 7 8 9 10

FOCUS

1 2 3 4 5 6 7 8 9 10

DISCIPLINE

1 2 3 4 5 6 7 8 9 10

NOTES:

List 3 WONDERFUL things that happened today:

List 3 CHALLENGES that you encountered today (if you had any):

What are some possible solutions to these challenges?

TIME

I have:

Final Thoughts:

DAY 14

Let's Go!

Do not do it for them. Do it for you!

While others might be motivators in your quest to obtain your health and fitness goal, ultimately do it for yourself.

You deserve it.

GOOD MORNING!

14

Date: ______________________

Hours Slept: ______________________

I am grateful for:

MYSELF:

OTHERS:

THINGS:

In 15 Days, I Will:

Thoughts/Brain Dump:

14

TO DO LIST

MUST DO	BONUS	DROP/DELEGATE

TASKS COMPLETED	TIME START	TIME FINISH
1.		
2.		
3.		
4.		
5.		

NUTRITION

14

Meal: am/pm

SUPPLEMENTS & WATER	PROTEIN	CARBS	FAT	OTHER

Meal: am/pm

SUPPLEMENTS & WATER	PROTEIN	CARBS	FAT	OTHER

Meal: am/pm

SUPPLEMENTS & WATER	PROTEIN	CARBS	FAT	OTHER

Meal: am/pm

SUPPLEMENTS & WATER	PROTEIN	CARBS	FAT	OTHER

Meal: am/pm

SUPPLEMENTS & WATER	PROTEIN	CARBS	FAT	OTHER

14

TRAINING

Workout:

EXERCISE	SETS	REPS	NOTES/WEIGHTS

CARDIO	TIME	NOTES

Workout Notes/Reflections:

SOCIAL MEDIA AWARENESS

14

What or who were you looking at?

How did it make you feel? (sad, mad, guilty, envious, happy, motivated, inspired, proud)

Was there something you did today that you refrained from posting online? Give yourself credit and write it down here!

How do you plan to use social media tomorrow?

14

NIGHT

ENERGY
1 2 3 4 5 6 7 8 9 10

MOOD
1 2 3 4 5 6 7 8 9 10

FOCUS
1 2 3 4 5 6 7 8 9 10

DISCIPLINE
1 2 3 4 5 6 7 8 9 10

NOTES:

List 3 WONDERFUL things that happened today:

List 3 CHALLENGES that you encountered today (if you had any):

What are some possible solutions to these challenges?

TIME

14

Am I closer to my goal?

✓

✗

I have:

Final Thoughts:

WEEK 2

WEEKLY

How many days did you workout?	
How were your eating habits this week?	
Did you skip any meals? (If so, how many?)	
Did you over-eat/binge?	
How many alcoholic beverages did you consume?	
What was one thing that you did for YOURSELF that no one else knows about?	
Did anyone do anything for you that you would like to take note of?	
How were your spending habits?	

REVIEW

WEEK 2

List 3 things that went well with your food/water/training this week:

How will you amplify these things this coming week?

List 3 things that went well, outside of your food/water/training this week:

How will you amplify these things this coming week?

2 WEEK

WEEKLY REVIEW

List 3 things that you struggled with this past week with food/water/training:

My plan to fix these struggles:

List 3 things that you struggled with this past week outside of your food/water/training:

My plan to fix these struggles:

NEXT WEEK'S FOCUS

I will:

Notes:

NOTES

NOTES

DAY 15

Let's Go!

Remember, you do not grow on your easiest days: you grow on your hardest days.

Even when you face challenges, they are opportunities to learn and grow.

You can do this!

GOOD MORNING!

15

Date: ______________________

Hours Slept: ________________

I am grateful for:

MYSELF:

OTHERS:

THINGS:

In 14 Days, I Will:

Thoughts/Brain Dump:

15

TO DO LIST

MUST DO	BONUS	DROP/DELEGATE

TASKS COMPLETED	TIME START	TIME FINISH
1.		
2.		
3.		
4.		
5.		

NUTRITION

15

Meal: **am/pm**

SUPPLEMENTS & WATER	PROTEIN	CARBS	FAT	OTHER

Meal: **am/pm**

SUPPLEMENTS & WATER	PROTEIN	CARBS	FAT	OTHER

Meal: **am/pm**

SUPPLEMENTS & WATER	PROTEIN	CARBS	FAT	OTHER

Meal: **am/pm**

SUPPLEMENTS & WATER	PROTEIN	CARBS	FAT	OTHER

Meal: **am/pm**

SUPPLEMENTS & WATER	PROTEIN	CARBS	FAT	OTHER

15

TRAINING

Workout:

EXERCISE	SETS	REPS	NOTES/WEIGHTS

CARDIO	TIME	NOTES

Workout Notes/Reflections:

SOCIAL MEDIA AWARENESS

15

What or who were you looking at?

How did it make you feel? (sad, mad, guilty, envious, happy, motivated, inspired, proud)

Was there something you did today that you refrained from posting online? Give yourself credit and write it down here!

How do you plan to use social media tomorrow?

15

NIGHT

ENERGY

1 2 3 4 5 6 7 8 9 10

MOOD

1 2 3 4 5 6 7 8 9 10

FOCUS

1 2 3 4 5 6 7 8 9 10

DISCIPLINE

1 2 3 4 5 6 7 8 9 10

NOTES:

List 3 WONDERFUL things that happened today:

List 3 CHALLENGES that you encountered today (if you had any):

What are some possible solutions to these challenges?

TIME 15

Am I closer to my goal?

I have:

Final Thoughts:

DAY 16

Let's Go!

Are you exercising today?

Remember, you do not have to go fast.

You just have to go!

GOOD MORNING!

16

Date: ______________________________

Hours Slept: ________________________

I am grateful for:

MYSELF:

OTHERS:

THINGS:

In 13 Days, I Will:

Thoughts/Brain Dump:

16

TO DO LIST

MUST DO	BONUS	DROP/DELEGATE

TASKS COMPLETED	TIME START	TIME FINISH
1.		
2.		
3.		
4.		
5.		

16

NUTRITION

Meal: am/pm

SUPPLEMENTS & WATER	PROTEIN	CARBS	FAT	OTHER

Meal: am/pm

SUPPLEMENTS & WATER	PROTEIN	CARBS	FAT	OTHER

Meal: am/pm

SUPPLEMENTS & WATER	PROTEIN	CARBS	FAT	OTHER

Meal: am/pm

SUPPLEMENTS & WATER	PROTEIN	CARBS	FAT	OTHER

Meal: am/pm

SUPPLEMENTS & WATER	PROTEIN	CARBS	FAT	OTHER

16

TRAINING

Workout:

EXERCISE	SETS	REPS	NOTES/WEIGHTS

CARDIO	TIME	NOTES

Workout Notes/Reflections:

SOCIAL MEDIA AWARENESS

16

What or who were you looking at?

How did it make you feel? (sad, mad, guilty, envious, happy, motivated, inspired, proud)

Was there something you did today that you refrained from posting online? Give yourself credit and write it down here!

How do you plan to use social media tomorrow?

16

NIGHT

ENERGY

1 2 3 4 5 6 7 8 9 10

MOOD

1 2 3 4 5 6 7 8 9 10

FOCUS

1 2 3 4 5 6 7 8 9 10

DISCIPLINE

1 2 3 4 5 6 7 8 9 10

NOTES:

List 3 WONDERFUL things that happened today:

List 3 CHALLENGES that you encountered today (if you had any):

What are some possible solutions to these challenges?

TIME

16

Am I closer to my goal?

✗

I have:

★ ★
★ ★
★ ★

Final Thoughts:

DAY 17
Let's Go!

Remember, dieting and training are not all-or-nothing. You may not be 100% perfect on your plan.

You are entitled to make mistakes, but you are NOT entitled to use those mistakes as excuses to throw in the towel.

17

GOOD MORNING!

Date: ______________________________

Hours Slept: ________________________

I am grateful for:

MYSELF:

OTHERS:

THINGS:

In 12 Days, I Will:

Thoughts/Brain Dump:

17

TO DO LIST

MUST DO	BONUS	DROP/DELEGATE

TASKS COMPLETED	TIME START	TIME FINISH
1.		
2.		
3.		
4.		
5.		

NUTRITION

Meal: am/pm

SUPPLEMENTS & WATER	PROTEIN	CARBS	FAT	OTHER

Meal: am/pm

SUPPLEMENTS & WATER	PROTEIN	CARBS	FAT	OTHER

Meal: am/pm

SUPPLEMENTS & WATER	PROTEIN	CARBS	FAT	OTHER

Meal: am/pm

SUPPLEMENTS & WATER	PROTEIN	CARBS	FAT	OTHER

Meal: am/pm

SUPPLEMENTS & WATER	PROTEIN	CARBS	FAT	OTHER

17

TRAINING

Workout:

EXERCISE	SETS	REPS	NOTES/WEIGHTS

CARDIO	TIME	NOTES

Workout Notes/Reflections:

17

SOCIAL MEDIA AWARENESS

What or who were you looking at?

How did it make you feel? (sad, mad, guilty, envious, happy, motivated, inspired, proud)

Was there something you did today that you refrained from posting online? Give yourself credit and write it down here!

How do you plan to use social media tomorrow?

17

NIGHT

ENERGY

1 2 3 4 5 6 7 8 9 10

MOOD

1 2 3 4 5 6 7 8 9 10

FOCUS

1 2 3 4 5 6 7 8 9 10

DISCIPLINE

1 2 3 4 5 6 7 8 9 10

NOTES:

List 3 WONDERFUL things that happened today:

List 3 CHALLENGES that you encountered today (if you had any):

What are some possible solutions to these challenges?

TIME

17

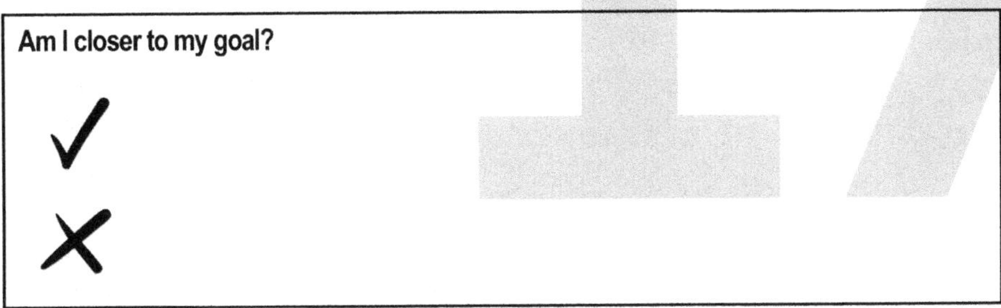

I have:

Final Thoughts:

DAY 18

Let's Go!

If you have been off track, take some time to reflect on just how good being on track and in control feels.

It is not always easy, but it always feels good at the end of the day.

GOOD MORNING!

18

Date: ________________________

Hours Slept: ____________________

I am grateful for:

MYSELF:

OTHERS:

THINGS:

In 11 Days, I Will:

Thoughts/Brain Dump:

18

TO DO LIST

MUST DO	BONUS	DROP/DELEGATE

TASKS COMPLETED	TIME START	TIME FINISH
1.		
2.		
3.		
4.		
5.		

NUTRITION

18

Meal: **am/pm**

SUPPLEMENTS & WATER	PROTEIN	CARBS	FAT	OTHER

Meal: **am/pm**

SUPPLEMENTS & WATER	PROTEIN	CARBS	FAT	OTHER

Meal: **am/pm**

SUPPLEMENTS & WATER	PROTEIN	CARBS	FAT	OTHER

Meal: **am/pm**

SUPPLEMENTS & WATER	PROTEIN	CARBS	FAT	OTHER

Meal: **am/pm**

SUPPLEMENTS & WATER	PROTEIN	CARBS	FAT	OTHER

18

TRAINING

Workout:

EXERCISE	SETS	REPS	NOTES/WEIGHTS

CARDIO	TIME	NOTES

Workout Notes/Reflections:

SOCIAL MEDIA AWARENESS

18

What or who were you looking at?

How did it make you feel? (sad, mad, guilty, envious, happy, motivated, inspired, proud)

Was there something you did today that you refrained from posting online? Give yourself credit and write it down here!

How do you plan to use social media tomorrow?

18

NIGHT

ENERGY

1 2 3 4 5 6 7 8 9 10

MOOD

1 2 3 4 5 6 7 8 9 10

FOCUS

1 2 3 4 5 6 7 8 9 10

DISCIPLINE

1 2 3 4 5 6 7 8 9 10

NOTES:

List 3 WONDERFUL things that happened today:

List 3 CHALLENGES that you encountered today (if you had any):

What are some possible solutions to these challenges?

TIME

18

Am I closer to my goal?

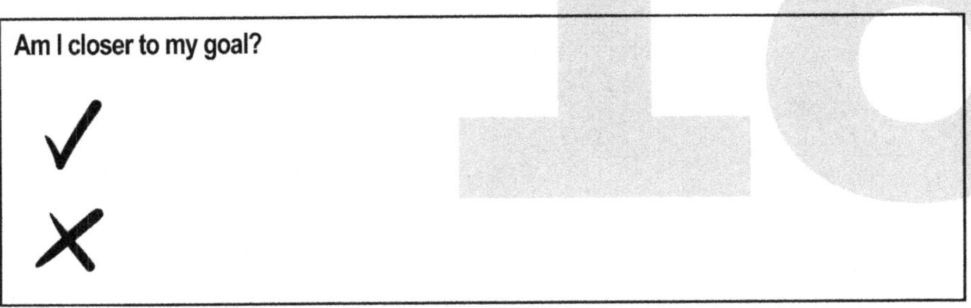

I have:

★

★

★

★

★

★

Final Thoughts:

DAY 19

Let's Go!

Instead of feeling burdened by having to eat healthfully and exercise, it is important to remember how LUCKY you are to be able to do these things.

GOOD MORNING!

19

Date: ______________________________

Hours Slept: ________________________

I am grateful for:

MYSELF:

OTHERS:

THINGS:

In 10 Days, I Will:

Thoughts/Brain Dump:

19

TO DO LIST

MUST DO	BONUS	DROP/DELEGATE

TASKS COMPLETED	TIME START	TIME FINISH
1.		
2.		
3.		
4.		
5.		

19

NUTRITION

Meal: **am/pm**

SUPPLEMENTS & WATER	PROTEIN	CARBS	FAT	OTHER

Meal: **am/pm**

SUPPLEMENTS & WATER	PROTEIN	CARBS	FAT	OTHER

Meal: **am/pm**

SUPPLEMENTS & WATER	PROTEIN	CARBS	FAT	OTHER

Meal: **am/pm**

SUPPLEMENTS & WATER	PROTEIN	CARBS	FAT	OTHER

Meal: **am/pm**

SUPPLEMENTS & WATER	PROTEIN	CARBS	FAT	OTHER

19

TRAINING

Workout:

EXERCISE	SETS	REPS	NOTES/WEIGHTS

CARDIO	TIME	NOTES

Workout Notes/Reflections:

19 SOCIAL MEDIA AWARENESS

What or who were you looking at?

How did it make you feel? (sad, mad, guilty, envious, happy, motivated, inspired, proud)

Was there something you did today that you refrained from posting online? Give yourself credit and write it down here!

How do you plan to use social media tomorrow?

19

NIGHT

ENERGY
1 2 3 4 5 6 7 8 9 10

MOOD
1 2 3 4 5 6 7 8 9 10

FOCUS
1 2 3 4 5 6 7 8 9 10

DISCIPLINE
1 2 3 4 5 6 7 8 9 10

NOTES:

List 3 WONDERFUL things that happened today:

List 3 CHALLENGES that you encountered today (if you had any):

What are some possible solutions to these challenges?

TIME

19

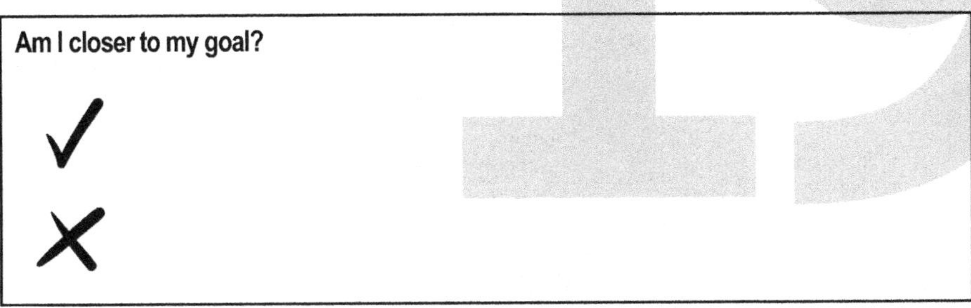

Am I closer to my goal?

✓

✗

I have:

Final Thoughts:

DAY 20

Let's Go!

On any given day, the number on the scale is exactly what it should be; given what you ate the day before, how much energy you expended, and various biological factors, etc.

Even if you were perfect on your diet, the scale may not go down due to a hundred different reasons.

GOOD MORNING!

20

Date: ____________________

Hours Slept: ________________

I am grateful for:

MYSELF:

OTHERS:

THINGS:

In 9 Days, I Will:

Thoughts/Brain Dump:

20

TO DO LIST

MUST DO	BONUS	DROP/DELEGATE

TASKS COMPLETED	TIME START	TIME FINISH
1.		
2.		
3.		
4.		
5.		

NUTRITION

20

Meal: am/pm

SUPPLEMENTS & WATER	PROTEIN	CARBS	FAT	OTHER

Meal: am/pm

SUPPLEMENTS & WATER	PROTEIN	CARBS	FAT	OTHER

Meal: am/pm

SUPPLEMENTS & WATER	PROTEIN	CARBS	FAT	OTHER

Meal: am/pm

SUPPLEMENTS & WATER	PROTEIN	CARBS	FAT	OTHER

Meal: am/pm

SUPPLEMENTS & WATER	PROTEIN	CARBS	FAT	OTHER

20

TRAINING

Workout:

EXERCISE	SETS	REPS	NOTES/WEIGHTS

CARDIO	TIME	NOTES

Workout Notes/Reflections:

20

SOCIAL MEDIA AWARENESS

What or who were you looking at?

How did it make you feel? (sad, mad, guilty, envious, happy, motivated, inspired, proud)

Was there something you did today that you refrained from posting online? Give yourself credit and write it down here!

How do you plan to use social media tomorrow?

20

NIGHT

ENERGY
1 2 3 4 5 6 7 8 9 10

MOOD
1 2 3 4 5 6 7 8 9 10

FOCUS
1 2 3 4 5 6 7 8 9 10

DISCIPLINE
1 2 3 4 5 6 7 8 9 10

NOTES:

List 3 WONDERFUL things that happened today:

List 3 CHALLENGES that you encountered today (if you had any):

What are some possible solutions to these challenges?

TIME 20

Am I closer to my goal?

✓

✗

I have:

★

★

★

★

★

★

Final Thoughts:

DAY 21
Let's Go!

Dieting and eating healthy can be hard—but that does not mean you cannot do it.

Likely, you have accomplished other hard things in your life that you were not sure you would be able to achieve.

Just because something can be hard to do, there is no excuse for you to not try.

GOOD MORNING!

21

Date: ______________________

Hours Slept: ______________________

I am grateful for:

MYSELF:

OTHERS:

THINGS:

In 8 Days, I Will:

Thoughts/Brain Dump:

21

TO DO LIST

MUST DO	BONUS	DROP/DELEGATE

TASKS COMPLETED	TIME START	TIME FINISH
1.		
2.		
3.		
4.		
5.		

NUTRITION

21

Meal: am/pm

SUPPLEMENTS & WATER	PROTEIN	CARBS	FAT	OTHER

Meal: am/pm

SUPPLEMENTS & WATER	PROTEIN	CARBS	FAT	OTHER

Meal: am/pm

SUPPLEMENTS & WATER	PROTEIN	CARBS	FAT	OTHER

Meal: am/pm

SUPPLEMENTS & WATER	PROTEIN	CARBS	FAT	OTHER

Meal: am/pm

SUPPLEMENTS & WATER	PROTEIN	CARBS	FAT	OTHER

21

TRAINING

Workout:

EXERCISE	SETS	REPS	NOTES/WEIGHTS

CARDIO	TIME	NOTES

Workout Notes/Reflections:

21

SOCIAL MEDIA AWARENESS

What or who were you looking at?

How did it make you feel? (sad, mad, guilty, envious, happy, motivated, inspired, proud)

Was there something you did today that you refrained from posting online? Give yourself credit and write it down here!

How do you plan to use social media tomorrow?

21

NIGHT

ENERGY
1 2 3 4 5 6 7 8 9 10

MOOD
1 2 3 4 5 6 7 8 9 10

FOCUS
1 2 3 4 5 6 7 8 9 10

DISCIPLINE
1 2 3 4 5 6 7 8 9 10

NOTES:

List 3 WONDERFUL things that happened today:

List 3 CHALLENGES that you encountered today (if you had any):

What are some possible solutions to these challenges?

TIME 21

Am I closer to my goal?

✓

✗

I have:

★

★

★

★

★

★

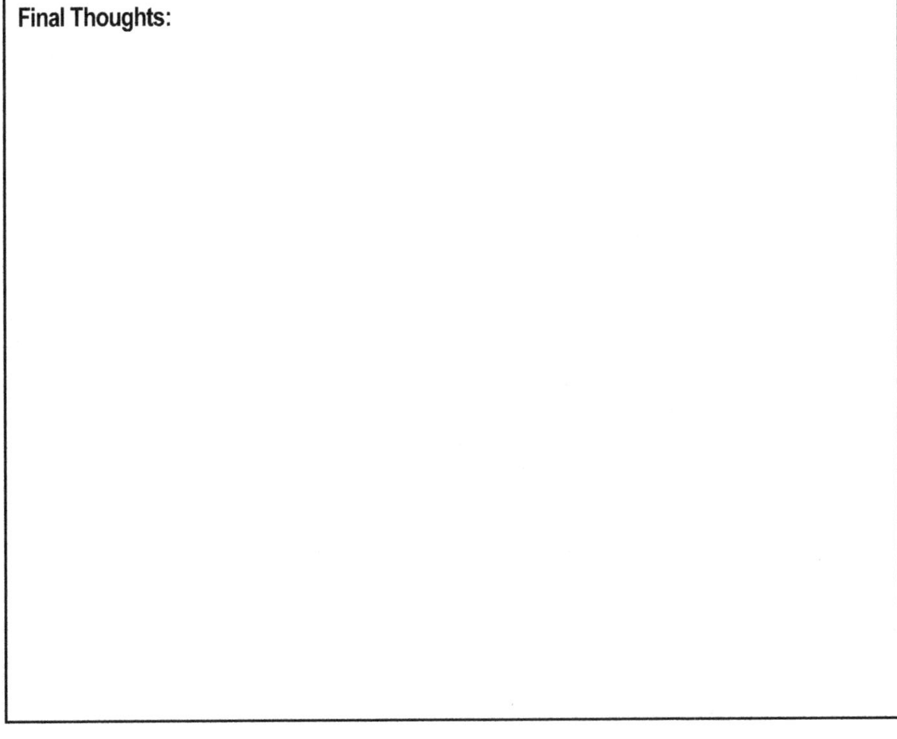

Final Thoughts:

WEEKLY

How many days did you workout?	
How were your eating habits this week?	
Did you skip any meals? (If so, how many?)	
Did you over-eat/binge?	
How many alcoholic beverages did you consume?	
What was one thing that you did for YOURSELF that no one else knows about?	
Did anyone do anything for you that you would like to take note of?	
How were your spending habits?	

REVIEW

List 3 things that went well with your food/water/training this week:

How will you amplify these things this coming week?

List 3 things that went well, outside of your food/water/training this week:

How will you amplify these things this coming week?

3 WEEK

WEEKLY REVIEW

List 3 things that you struggled with this past week with food/water/training:

My plan to fix these struggles:

List 3 things that you struggled with this past week outside of your food/water/training:

My plan to fix these struggles:

NEXT WEEK'S FOCUS

NOTES

NOTES

DAY 22
Let's Go!

If you work on staying in control of your eating, not only will you feel good about yourself and your eating; but doing so will also help you reach your health and fitness goals.

GOOD MORNING!

22

Date: ____________________________

Hours Slept: ______________________

I am grateful for:

MYSELF:

OTHERS:

THINGS:

In 7 Days, I Will:

Thoughts/Brain Dump:

22

TO DO LIST

MUST DO	BONUS	DROP/DELEGATE

TASKS COMPLETED	TIME START	TIME FINISH
1.		
2.		
3.		
4.		
5.		

NUTRITION

22

Meal: am/pm

SUPPLEMENTS & WATER	PROTEIN	CARBS	FAT	OTHER

Meal: am/pm

SUPPLEMENTS & WATER	PROTEIN	CARBS	FAT	OTHER

Meal: am/pm

SUPPLEMENTS & WATER	PROTEIN	CARBS	FAT	OTHER

Meal: am/pm

SUPPLEMENTS & WATER	PROTEIN	CARBS	FAT	OTHER

Meal: am/pm

SUPPLEMENTS & WATER	PROTEIN	CARBS	FAT	OTHER

22

TRAINING

Workout:

EXERCISE	SETS	REPS	NOTES/WEIGHTS

CARDIO	TIME	NOTES

Workout Notes/Reflections:

SOCIAL MEDIA AWARENESS

22

What or who were you looking at?

How did it make you feel? (sad, mad, guilty, envious, happy, motivated, inspired, proud)

Was there something you did today that you refrained from posting online? Give yourself credit and write it down here!

How do you plan to use social media tomorrow?

22

NIGHT

ENERGY
1 2 3 4 5 6 7 8 9 10

MOOD
1 2 3 4 5 6 7 8 9 10

FOCUS
1 2 3 4 5 6 7 8 9 10

DISCIPLINE
1 2 3 4 5 6 7 8 9 10

NOTES:

List 3 WONDERFUL things that happened today:

List 3 CHALLENGES that you encountered today (if you had any):

What are some possible solutions to these challenges?

TIME 22

Am I closer to my goal?

I have:

Final Thoughts:

DAY 23

Let's Go!

If you feel your motivation dropping, take a moment to think about all the reasons why it is worthwhile to stick to the goals you have set for yourself.

Ask yourself, "Since these are such important goals, do they merit hard work and extra effort? Are they important enough to not give up on?" Then, re-commit yourself and get going!

GOOD MORNING!

23

Date: ______________________

Hours Slept: ______________________

I am grateful for:

MYSELF:

OTHERS:

THINGS:

In 6 Days, I Will:

Thoughts/Brain Dump:

23

TO DO LIST

MUST DO	BONUS	DROP/DELEGATE

TASKS COMPLETED	TIME START	TIME FINISH
1.		
2.		
3.		
4.		
5.		

NUTRITION

23

Meal: **am/pm**

SUPPLEMENTS & WATER	PROTEIN	CARBS	FAT	OTHER

Meal: **am/pm**

SUPPLEMENTS & WATER	PROTEIN	CARBS	FAT	OTHER

Meal: **am/pm**

SUPPLEMENTS & WATER	PROTEIN	CARBS	FAT	OTHER

Meal: **am/pm**

SUPPLEMENTS & WATER	PROTEIN	CARBS	FAT	OTHER

Meal: **am/pm**

SUPPLEMENTS & WATER	PROTEIN	CARBS	FAT	OTHER

23

TRAINING

Workout:

EXERCISE	SETS	REPS	NOTES/WEIGHTS

CARDIO	TIME	NOTES

Workout Notes/Reflections:

SOCIAL MEDIA AWARENESS

23

What or who were you looking at?

How did it make you feel? (sad, mad, guilty, envious, happy, motivated, inspired, proud)

Was there something you did today that you refrained from posting online? Give yourself credit and write it down here!

How do you plan to use social media tomorrow?

23

NIGHT

ENERGY
1 2 3 4 5 6 7 8 9 10

MOOD
1 2 3 4 5 6 7 8 9 10

FOCUS
1 2 3 4 5 6 7 8 9 10

DISCIPLINE
1 2 3 4 5 6 7 8 9 10

NOTES:

List 3 WONDERFUL things that happened today:

List 3 CHALLENGES that you encountered today (if you had any):

What are some possible solutions to these challenges?

TIME

Am I closer to my goal?

✓

✗

I have:

★

★

★

★

★

★

Final Thoughts:

DAY 24

Let's Go!

Cravings are about want, not need.

When you think "I really need this food right now.", remind yourself "Actually, I really want this food right now, but I want all the benefits of my goals so much more. It is worth it to resist because it will get me to my goals."

GOOD MORNING!

24

Date: ___________________________

Hours Slept: ______________________

I am grateful for:

MYSELF:

OTHERS:

THINGS:

In 5 Days, I Will:

Thoughts/Brain Dump:

24

TO DO LIST

MUST DO	BONUS	DROP/DELEGATE

TASKS COMPLETED	TIME START	TIME FINISH
1.		
2.		
3.		
4.		
5.		

NUTRITION

24

Meal: am/pm

SUPPLEMENTS & WATER	PROTEIN	CARBS	FAT	OTHER

Meal: am/pm

SUPPLEMENTS & WATER	PROTEIN	CARBS	FAT	OTHER

Meal: am/pm

SUPPLEMENTS & WATER	PROTEIN	CARBS	FAT	OTHER

Meal: am/pm

SUPPLEMENTS & WATER	PROTEIN	CARBS	FAT	OTHER

Meal: am/pm

SUPPLEMENTS & WATER	PROTEIN	CARBS	FAT	OTHER

24

TRAINING

Workout:

EXERCISE	SETS	REPS	NOTES/WEIGHTS

CARDIO	TIME	NOTES

Workout Notes/Reflections:

SOCIAL MEDIA AWARENESS

24

What or who were you looking at?

How did it make you feel? (sad, mad, guilty, envious, happy, motivated, inspired, proud)

Was there something you did today that you refrained from posting online? Give yourself credit and write it down here!

How do you plan to use social media tomorrow?

24

NIGHT

ENERGY
1 2 3 4 5 6 7 8 9 10

MOOD
1 2 3 4 5 6 7 8 9 10

FOCUS
1 2 3 4 5 6 7 8 9 10

DISCIPLINE
1 2 3 4 5 6 7 8 9 10

NOTES:

List 3 **WONDERFUL** things that happened today:

List 3 **CHALLENGES** that you encountered today (if you had any):

What are some possible solutions to these challenges?

TIME 24

Am I closer to my goal?

I have:

★

★

★

★

★

★

Final Thoughts:

DAY 25

Let's Go!

Everybody makes mistakes.

You are entitled to make mistakes—but you are not entitled to let the memory of those mistakes get in your way.

Wipe your slate clean and re-focus right this moment!

NUTRITION

25

Meal: **am/pm**

SUPPLEMENTS & WATER	PROTEIN	CARBS	FAT	OTHER

Meal: **am/pm**

SUPPLEMENTS & WATER	PROTEIN	CARBS	FAT	OTHER

Meal: **am/pm**

SUPPLEMENTS & WATER	PROTEIN	CARBS	FAT	OTHER

Meal: **am/pm**

SUPPLEMENTS & WATER	PROTEIN	CARBS	FAT	OTHER

Meal: **am/pm**

SUPPLEMENTS & WATER	PROTEIN	CARBS	FAT	OTHER

25

TRAINING

Workout:

EXERCISE	SETS	REPS	NOTES/WEIGHTS

CARDIO	TIME	NOTES

Workout Notes/Reflections:

SOCIAL MEDIA AWARENESS

25

What or who were you looking at?

How did it make you feel? (sad, mad, guilty, envious, happy, motivated, inspired, proud)

Was there something you did today that you refrained from posting online? Give yourself credit and write it down here!

How do you plan to use social media tomorrow?

25

NIGHT

ENERGY
1 2 3 4 5 6 7 8 9 10

MOOD
1 2 3 4 5 6 7 8 9 10

FOCUS
1 2 3 4 5 6 7 8 9 10

DISCIPLINE
1 2 3 4 5 6 7 8 9 10

NOTES:

List 3 WONDERFUL things that happened today:

List 3 CHALLENGES that you encountered today (if you had any):

What are some possible solutions to these challenges?

TIME

I have:

★ ★

★ ★

★ ★

Final Thoughts:

DAY 26

Let's Go!

If you think "I will start back tomorrow.", remind yourself that today is yesterday's tomorrow, which means that tomorrow is today and it is time to get started RIGHT NOW!

GOOD MORNING!

26

Date: ______________________

Hours Slept: ______________________

I am grateful for:

MYSELF:

OTHERS:

THINGS:

In 3 Days, I Will:

Thoughts/Brain Dump:

26

TO DO LIST

MUST DO	BONUS	DROP/DELEGATE

TASKS COMPLETED	TIME START	TIME FINISH
1.		
2.		
3.		
4.		
5.		

NUTRITION

26

Meal: **am/pm**

SUPPLEMENTS & WATER	PROTEIN	CARBS	FAT	OTHER

Meal: **am/pm**

SUPPLEMENTS & WATER	PROTEIN	CARBS	FAT	OTHER

Meal: **am/pm**

SUPPLEMENTS & WATER	PROTEIN	CARBS	FAT	OTHER

Meal: **am/pm**

SUPPLEMENTS & WATER	PROTEIN	CARBS	FAT	OTHER

Meal: **am/pm**

SUPPLEMENTS & WATER	PROTEIN	CARBS	FAT	OTHER

26

TRAINING

Workout:

EXERCISE	SETS	REPS	NOTES/WEIGHTS

CARDIO	TIME	NOTES

Workout Notes/Reflections:

SOCIAL MEDIA AWARENESS

26

What or who were you looking at?

How did it make you feel? (sad, mad, guilty, envious, happy, motivated, inspired, proud)

Was there something you did today that you refrained from posting online? Give yourself credit and write it down here!

How do you plan to use social media tomorrow?

26

NIGHT

ENERGY
1 2 3 4 5 6 7 8 9 10

MOOD
1 2 3 4 5 6 7 8 9 10

FOCUS
1 2 3 4 5 6 7 8 9 10

DISCIPLINE
1 2 3 4 5 6 7 8 9 10

NOTES:

List 3 WONDERFUL things that happened today:

List 3 CHALLENGES that you encountered today (if you had any):

What are some possible solutions to these challenges?

TIME

26

DAY 27

Let's Go!

You cannot always stop sabotaging thoughts from occurring, but you can control whether or not you give in and let them derail you.

Remember, it does not mean it is 100% true just because you think it.

GOOD MORNING!

27

Date: ____________________

Hours Slept: ____________________

I am grateful for:

MYSELF:

OTHERS:

THINGS:

In 2 Days, I Will:

Thoughts/Brain Dump:

27

TO DO LIST

MUST DO	BONUS	DROP/DELEGATE

TASKS COMPLETED	TIME START	TIME FINISH
1.		
2.		
3.		
4.		
5.		

NUTRITION

27

Meal: **am/pm**

SUPPLEMENTS & WATER	PROTEIN	CARBS	FAT	OTHER

Meal: **am/pm**

SUPPLEMENTS & WATER	PROTEIN	CARBS	FAT	OTHER

Meal: **am/pm**

SUPPLEMENTS & WATER	PROTEIN	CARBS	FAT	OTHER

Meal: **am/pm**

SUPPLEMENTS & WATER	PROTEIN	CARBS	FAT	OTHER

Meal: **am/pm**

SUPPLEMENTS & WATER	PROTEIN	CARBS	FAT	OTHER

27 TRAINING

Workout:

EXERCISE	SETS	REPS	NOTES/WEIGHTS

CARDIO	TIME	NOTES

Workout Notes/Reflections:

SOCIAL MEDIA AWARENESS

27

What or who were you looking at?

How did it make you feel? (sad, mad, guilty, envious, happy, motivated, inspired, proud)

Was there something you did today that you refrained from posting online? Give yourself credit and write it down here!

How do you plan to use social media tomorrow?

27

NIGHT

ENERGY
1 2 3 4 5 6 7 8 9 10

MOOD
1 2 3 4 5 6 7 8 9 10

FOCUS
1 2 3 4 5 6 7 8 9 10

DISCIPLINE
1 2 3 4 5 6 7 8 9 10

NOTES:

List 3 WONDERFUL things that happened today:

List 3 CHALLENGES that you encountered today (if you had any):

What are some possible solutions to these challenges?

TIME 27

Am I closer to my goal?

✓

✗

I have:

★ ★
★ ★
★ ★

Final Thoughts:

DAY 28
Let's Go!

Success and maintenance in health and fitness are combinations of all the small things you do in a day, not a result of any one big thing.

That is why it is important to give yourself credit for every big AND small thing you do well!

GOOD MORNING!

28

Date: ______________________________

Hours Slept: ________________________

I am grateful for:

MYSELF:

OTHERS:

THINGS:

In 1 Day, I Will:

Thoughts/Brain Dump:

28

TO DO LIST

MUST DO	BONUS	DROP/DELEGATE

TASKS COMPLETED	TIME START	TIME FINISH
1.		
2.		
3.		
4.		
5.		

NUTRITION

28

Meal: am/pm

SUPPLEMENTS & WATER	PROTEIN	CARBS	FAT	OTHER

Meal: am/pm

SUPPLEMENTS & WATER	PROTEIN	CARBS	FAT	OTHER

Meal: am/pm

SUPPLEMENTS & WATER	PROTEIN	CARBS	FAT	OTHER

Meal: am/pm

SUPPLEMENTS & WATER	PROTEIN	CARBS	FAT	OTHER

Meal: am/pm

SUPPLEMENTS & WATER	PROTEIN	CARBS	FAT	OTHER

28 TRAINING

Workout:

EXERCISE	SETS	REPS	NOTES/WEIGHTS

CARDIO	TIME	NOTES

Workout Notes/Reflections:

SOCIAL MEDIA AWARENESS

28

What or who were you looking at?

How did it make you feel? (sad, mad, guilty, envious, happy, motivated, inspired, proud)

Was there something you did today that you refrained from posting online? Give yourself credit and write it down here!

How do you plan to use social media tomorrow?

28

NIGHT

ENERGY

1 2 3 4 5 6 7 8 9 10

MOOD

1 2 3 4 5 6 7 8 9 10

FOCUS

1 2 3 4 5 6 7 8 9 10

DISCIPLINE

1 2 3 4 5 6 7 8 9 10

NOTES:

List 3 WONDERFUL things that happened today:

List 3 CHALLENGES that you encountered today (if you had any):

What are some possible solutions to these challenges?

TIME

28

4 WEEK

WEEKLY

How many days did you workout?	
How were your eating habits this week?	
Did you skip any meals? (If so, how many?)	
Did you over-eat/binge?	
How many alcoholic beverages did you consume?	
What was one thing that you did for YOURSELF that no one else knows about?	
Did anyone do anything for you that you would like to take note of?	
How were your spending habits?	

REVIEW

List 3 things that went well with your food/water/training this week:

How will you amplify these things this coming week?

List 3 things that went well, outside of your food/water/training this week:

How will you amplify these things this coming week?

4 WEEK

WEEKLY REVIEW

List 3 things that you struggled with this past week with food/water/training:

My plan to fix these struggles:

List 3 things that you struggled with this past week outside of your food/water/training:

My plan to fix these struggles:

NEXT WEEK'S FOCUS

NOTES

NOTES

YOU DID IT!

Congrats!

REACHING MY GOAL

Did you accomplish your original goal? Or did it change?

What were some of the best habits you created over the past 4 weeks?

What were some of the biggest lessons you learned from using this journal?

REACHING MY GOAL

How are you different from 4 weeks ago?

What are you going to continue to do moving forward?

My goal for the next 28 days is:

WHAT I SEE IN THE MIRROR

DO NOT LOOK AT YOUR PREVIOUS DRAWING BEFORE CONDUCTING THIS EXERCISE!

In the space below, draw a NEW self portrait. From head to toe, draw what you perceive yourself to be—now that you have concluded the 4 week journal. When finished, have a look at the first one and see what differences there are now!

MY NEW ROUTINE

4am

5am

6am

7am

8am

9am

10am

11am

12pm

1pm

2pm

3pm

4pm

5pm

6pm

7pm

8pm

9pm

10pm

11pm

12am

1am

2am

3am

NOTES